the Mac OS X
conversion kit:

9 to 10 side by side

Scott Kelby

Mac OS X Conversion Kit

The Mac OS X
Conversion Kit Team

EDITOR
Richard Theriault

TECHNICAL EDITOR
Lesa Snider

COPY EDITOR
Kim Gabriel

PRODUCTION
Dave Gales
Paul Royka
Margie Rosenstein

COVER DESIGN AND
CREATIVE CONCEPTS
Felix Nelson

SITE DESIGN
Stacy Behan

The Peachpit Team

ASSOCIATE PUBLISHER
Stepanie Wall

EXECUTIVE EDITOR
Steve Weiss

PRODUCTION MANAGER
Gina Kanouse

SENIOR PROJECT EDITOR
Kristy Knoop

COMPOSITOR
Gloria Schurick

PUBLISHED BY
Peachpit Press

Copyright © 2003 by Peachpit Press

FIRST EDITION: June 2003

International Standard Book Number: 0-7357-1354-5

Library of Congress Catalog Card Number: 200217493

05 04 03   7 6 5 4 3 2

Interpretation of the printing code: The rightmost double-digit number is the year of the book's printing; the rightmost single-digit number is the number of the book's printing. For example, the printing code 03-1 shows that the first printing of the book occurred in 2003.

Composed in Myriad and Helvetica by NAPP Publishing

Printed in the United States of America

Trademarks
All terms mentioned in this book that are known to be trademarks or service marks have been appropriately capitalized. Peachpit Press cannot attest to the accuracy of this information. Use of a term in the book should not be regarded as affecting the validity of any trademark or service mark.

Macintosh and Mac are registered trademarks of Apple Computer.

Warning and Disclaimer
This book is designed to provide information about Mac OS X. Every effort has been made to make this book as complete and as accurate as possible, but no warranty of fitness is implied.

The information is provided on an as-is basis. The authors and Peachpit Press shall have neither liability nor responsibility to any person or entity with respect to any loss or damages arising from the information contained in this book or from the use of the discs or programs that may accompany it.

www.peachpit.com
www.scottkelbybooks.com

For my "Mac Buddies":
Bill Carroll, Don Wiggins, Jim Patterson, Rod Harlan,
Jim Workman, Dick Theriault, Ken Pitt, Dave Moser, Lesa Snider, Terry White,
Dave Gales, Jim Nordquist, John Couch, Larry Becker, Jon Gales, Jim Goodman
and all my friends at the Bay Area Macintosh Users Group (BAM).

Acknowledgments

Putting together a book like this takes a team of very talented, creative, and dedicated people. Not only did I have the good fortune of working with such a great group of Mac-loving fanatics, I now get the great pleasure of thanking them, and acknowledging their hard work and tireless dedication.

First I'd like to thank my beautiful and amazing wife Kalebra, for putting a smile on my lips, and a song in my heart, each and every day. She's part wonderwoman, part supermom, part business exec and part stand-up comic. She makes every day a wonderful new experience, and I'm the luckiest guy in the world to have her.

I also want to thank my son Jordan. He's my special "little buddy" who's graced with his mom's smile, her love of life, and her true loving heart. The two of them bring an immeasureable amount of joy into my life and I'm very grateful God has blessed me with them.

Special thanks go to my contributing author Dave Gales, whose invaluable contributions to the book helped make it better in so many ways. Thanks for all your research, organizational skills, creative ideas, and dedication to the project.

To Dave Moser, for convincing me a few years ago to go beyond writing pro-Mac articles, and start writing pro-Mac books.

To Felix Nelson, for his ideas, his input, his great cover art, and for lending his overall creative talents to this book.

To the action-packed Lesa Snider (a.k.a. "the Yellow Rose of Texas") for agreeing to tech edit the book in the midst of a dozen other projects. Clearly, she is a "Love Otter."

To Dick Theriault, the royal Macintosh book editor, for his priceless contributions to the book, and for once again letting us pull him kicking and screaming out of retirement.

Thanks to my editor Steve Weiss at Peachpit Publishing. It takes a measureable amount of guts to publish a book that steps outside the boundaries of traditional Mac books, and my hat's off to him for having the vision to see where and how it fits in, and for his singular vision of "just wanting to make great books." Also, special thanks to Rachel Tiley at New Riders, an unsung hero of book publishing.

I couldn't do any of this without the help and support of my wonderful assistant Kathy Siler. She's got an amazing attitude, except during football season when the Redskins are losing, which is fairly often as of late, but that's clearly not my fault.

To my brother Jeff, for being such an important part of my life, for becoming a part of our team, and for being a brother all other brothers should be judged by. You da man!

To Paul Royka and Margie Rosenstein for making the layout squeaky clean, and to Kim Gabriel for organizing the whole thing, and giving all the words another good workout.

Thanks to the whole team at KW Media Group, for their committment to excellence, for refusing to accept limitations, and for being an example of what's best about this industry.

To my friends and business partners Jim Workman and Jean A. Kendra for their support and enthusiasm for all my writing projects.

And most importantly, an extra special thanks to God and His son Jesus Christ for always hearing my prayers, for always being there when I need Him, and for blessing me with a wonderful life I truly love, and such a warm, loving family to share it with.

About The Author

Scott Kelby

Scott is Editor-in-Chief and co-founder of Mac Design Magazine, *Editor-in-Chief of* Photoshop User *magazine, and president of the National Association of Photoshop Professionals, the trade association for Adobe® Photoshop® users. Scott is also president of KW Media Group, Inc., a Florida-based software training and publishing firm.*

Scott is author of the books Macintosh: The Naked Truth, Mac OS X Killer Tips, Photoshop 7 Down & Dirty Tricks, The Photoshop Book for Digital Photographers, *and* Photoshop 7 Killer Tips, *all from New Riders Publishing. He's a contributing author to the books* Photoshop Effects Magic, *also from New Riders;* Maclopedia, the Ultimate Reference on Everything Macintosh *from Hayden Books; and* Adobe Web Design and Publishing Unleashed *from Sams.net Publishing.*

Scott is Training Director for the Adobe Photoshop Seminar Tour, Technical Conference Chair for the Mac Design Conference and he is a speaker at graphics trade shows and events around the world. Scott is also featured in a series of Adobe Photoshop video training tapes and DVDs and has been training Mac users and graphics professionals since 1993.

For more background info visit www.scottkelby.com.

Contributing Author

Dave Gales

Dave is Systems Coordinator for KW Media Group, a Florida-based software training and publishing firm. He helps produce the Adobe Photoshop Seminar Tour, as well as the PhotoshopWorld conference (the annual convention of the National Association of Photoshop Professionals).

Dave is also founder and president of LifeMap Media, a creative firm that develops rich media resources and creative graphics for churches and small businesses. As president, he is able to combine his 20 years of experience as a local church pastor, his passion for clearly communicating God's story, his background as a professional photographer, and his long-time love for gadgets—Macintosh computers in particular—to create working solutions for the firm's clients.

T a b l e o f Contents

Table of Contents

Chapter Three   **56**

Customizing Your Mac
SETTING UP YOUR SYSTEM TO YOUR TASTE

Chapter Four   **82**

Crank Up the Jams
MUSIC, PHOTOS, AND VIDEO

Table of Contents

Chapter Eight   **164**

Other Stuff
THE LAND OF LITTLE LOST COMMANDS

Chapter Nine   **196**

Troubleshooting
IT'S NOT A GOOD SIGN IF YOU'RE READING THIS

Table of Contents

Chapter Twelve   **250**

20 Little Things Apple Changed Just to Mess with Your Head

ACTUALLY, THERE'S A METHOD BEHIND THEIR MADNESS.
AT LEAST THAT'S WHAT WE'VE BEEN LED TO BELIEVE.

Start Here
(Or face the consequences)

Does the world really need another Mac OS X book?
I had to ask myself the exact same question. After days of careful research and hours of intense and personal soul searching, I came to the conclusion that yes, the world does need at least one more Mac OS X book. This book. However, after this book is written, it will then be OK for federal officials to close the Mac OS X book market, allowing no more Mac OS X books to be written (unless it is determined by a unbiased board, made up of myself and a hand-picked group of my closest friends and family members, that indeed another Mac OS X book is necessary).

Why this book?
Because it's different, and handles things from a different perspective that will help different people in a different way (are you picking up a theme here?). Here's what I mean: In my opinion, David Pogue's *Mac OS X: The Missing Manual* is the best book out there for learning Mac OS X. It's so complete, so thorough (at over 700 pages), and so well written that it really has no peer. So it would be pretty dumb for me to write that kind of book—the "best of breed" is already out there. But there is a book missing. A book for people who don't have the time to read David's book and take advantage of its depth. A book for people who need to start actually using Mac OS X today, and then sometime down the road (next week, next month, etc.), they'll get around to learning all the ins and outs; but for today, they just need to get up and around in Mac OS X.

Who are these people? People like my wife. She was part of the inspiration for this book, because after years of using various and sundry versions of Mac OS 7, 8, and 9, she finally up-graded to OS X (solely to take advantage of iPhoto, and the built-in ease of downloading photos from her Nikon digital camera).

Well, once it was installed she went right to work, and within a few minutes she starting asking the usual questions—"Where's the Trash Can?" "Where are the Control Panels?" "How do I set the time?" and so on. I told her, "Honey, I've got a copy of David Pogue's book; you can read it tonight." She looked at me with total disdain, and said, "Do I really have to read a whole book? I didn't read a book to learn OS 9, can't you just show me?" This isn't the kind of thing an author likes to hear from his wife, so I tried to convince her it would be easy: "Sweetie, it's a great book, just spend a few hours with it." She gave me that "You don't get it" look, so I just answered a few more of her questions as they came up. More stuff along the lines of "Where'd they move the DVD player?" to "How do I change the system volume?" until finally she said something that changed everything. She said, "Ya know, you should write a book that just shows how to do the things you used to do in 9, but how to do them in X."

She's not nearly the Mac geek that I am, and even though I could put into her hands a copy of David's book that we already own, she just wouldn't read it, because she simply doesn't care. She needs to know the handful of things she wants to know, and outside of that, she just doesn't care. She doesn't care that there's a utility for setting your MIDI devices, or that there's a System Preference for remapping your keyboard to Croatian. She just wants to do what she always did in 9, but now she wants to do it in X. It makes perfect sense. I think, as Mac authors, we generally write books that we would buy—books for Mac geeks who want to know all the tiniest little details, because we love this stuff. We crave it, we eat it up, we can't get enough. On the other hand, my wife (and countless others like her) *can* get enough. This book is for them. Well, not just for them, it's also for people who will buy a book like David's (timesaving tip: just buy David's) and read it at their leisure to uncover all the magic of X. But for now, they just need to get up and running right away. This is the definitive "Get up and running right away" Mac OS X book for OS 8/9 users. It's actually the perfect complement to David's *Missing Manual* (but remember, if you can only buy one, buy mine—because at this point David probably has more money than Belgium's gross national product).

So what makes this book different?
I knew you where going to ask that. Well, first off, this book has a very specific audience—people who are familiar with Mac OS 8 or 9. If you just bought your first Mac—this book isn't for you, because you need to have already used Mac OS 8 or 9 to get anything out of it. Secondly, this book doesn't tell you everything about Mac OS X. In fact, it tells you only a small amount—just what you need to know, to do in Mac OS X the same things you did back in Mac OS 9.

Is this book for you?
That depends. Do you have $29.99? (Kidding. Sort of). Actually, it's for you if you need to start using Mac OS X today, and you can wait to learn all of the hidden, advanced, and cool other things it can do until some other time that's more convenient for you. Now, will I tell anyone if that time never comes? No. Your secret's safe with me. However, Mac OS X is pretty darn amazing, and by only reading this book, you'd be depriving yourself of learning from other great books, like the bestselling *Mac OS X Killer Tips*, from my favorite author (me), published by New Riders Publishing (ISBN: 0735713170).

Is this book for switchers?
Nope. This is NOT designed for people switching from PCs to Macs. This book is ONLY for people already using Macs and some version of Mac OS 8 or 9.

Oh come on , please?
No.

What if I am willing to pay more than the cover price?
Well, now. . . . No, no I can't do it. It's a specific book for specific people (speaking specifically).

Do you have to read the book in any order?
Absolutely not. I organized the book by topic, so you can use it more like a reference manual. For example, if you need to know how to adjust the brightness of your monitor, look in the Table of Contents, in the Monitors chapter. Remember, this book is there as your buddy, to help you find the things you're looking for in Mac OS X. So don't sit down and read it cover-to-cover. Instead, just keep it by your Mac, and at the first sign of "Hmmmm, where did they put that?" just grab the book and the answer is seconds away.

What if I'm installing Mac OS X myself?

Good luck! Actually, the installation process is very easy—it's having the answers to the questions that the Mac OS X Installer Assistant asks you along the way that is tricky. Although this book was designed to pick up after the installation (using Mac OS X, not installing it), I did include some things from the installation process that, if nothing more, might keep you from reaching a level of frustration that sends you climbing into a tower with a high-powered rifle and picking off pedestrians. Just look near the back of the book for Chapter 10 titled "Don't Freak Out".

How to use this book

It's very important to me that you get the most from this book, and to do that you have to "get inside my head." (Don't worry, there's plenty of room in there, because I have a spacious über head, which can comfortably accommodate a typical family of four.)

I put this book together from a Mac OS 9 user's point of view, so for example there's a chapter called "Monitors" because that's what Mac OS 9 users refer to their monitor as—a monitor (even though Apple now calls your monitor a "Display" in Mac OS X).

So, to use this book, just turn to the page that has the thing that you want to do in 9. On the left page, it shows (simply as a reminder) how you used to do that task in Mac OS 9, and the right page shows you how you do that same task now in Mac OS X. If Mac OS X offers some new features for that particular task (and it many cases it does), I included those at the bottom in a little call-out box named "new stuff" (quite a striking name, dontchathink?).

Also, although this book will work almost equally as well for Mac OS 8.5, 8.6, 9.0, 9.1, and 9.2 users (because those OS versions are all so similar), for the sake of sheer brevity, I always refer to the "old version" as Mac OS 9.

One more organizational thing: some techniques appear twice (giving you a déjà vu effect). That's because I figured you might go looking in different places for different things. I'd rather have you see something twice than have you miss seeing it.

What about the scary UNIX stuff?

This book contains no scary UNIX stuff. Since there was no UNIX in Mac OS 8/9, I can't show you how to do it in Mac OS X. Remember, this book is "how to do what you did in Mac OS 8/9, in Mac OS X." If it wasn't in Mac OS 9, it's not in this book. Except....

Except what?

Well, except I wanted to whet your appetite for some of the cool things Mac OS X can do, so I included Chapter 11 called "20 Cool Little Things You Couldn't Do in Mac OS 9." I also included Chapter 12 called "20 Little Things Apple Changed Just to Mess with Your Head." I also included some Quick Reference pages, with shortcuts to get you right where you want to go, after you've had a chance to work with the book a little bit. See, I care.

Is it time?

It's time. Have at it. Dive right in. Etc.

Chapter One

 Legend has it that deep beneath Apple's Cupertino, California headquarters is a hidden cave where members of a secret cult of Apple system engineers don their sacred gowns for their trip deep into the darkest hidden passageway to reach

The Apple Menu
THERE IS ONE, JUST NOT THE ONE YOU REMEMBER

"the weirding room." Stories are told of meetings where they gather in a circle, and one engineer whispers the name of a deeply loved and respected aspect of the Apple Operating System, and they all begin to laugh that we're-deep-in-a-secret-cave laugh that only people deep in a secret cave can laugh. Then they begin their ritual "changing the command" chant, where they each try to conjure up the most hideous, most insidious, yet deceivingly clever change they could implement that would cause nothing short of certain madness for longtime Macintosh users. The most famous of these sacred gatherings is the one where supposedly the engineer in the center of the ring whispered, "New folder shortcut," then after the appropriate amount of sinister cackling and macabre laughter, one engineer stood in the light of the flickering torches and said, "Let's make them add the Shift key (they all gasped), but better yet, let's use the *old* keyboard shortcut to open a new Finder window. Surely, my brothers, this will have the desired effect." They stood, cheered, and waved their chunks of freshly killed swine in the air. This engineer then became their king. And that's why today, even some of the most time-honored shortcuts and features have been changed, and that's exactly why this chapter exists: to show you where they've moved to now (by secret decree).

Apple Menu Options OS 9

Back in OS 9, you didn't have a lot of options for how your Apple Menu worked. Basically, if you went under the Apple menu, into the Control Panels folder, and chose Apple Menu Options, you got the Control Panel shown above. This let you turn on/off submenus, and let you determine how many recently used documents, applications, and servers would be displayed within the appropriate folders in the Apple menu. Pretty exciting stuff.

[Are Now] Dock Options OS X

OS X: Now that the Dock has replaced the old Apple menu, you have a host of options in-cluding control over the Dock's size, whether the icons magnify when you roll your mouse over them, and even the Dock's position on your screen. You can choose which effect will be used when you minimize a window to the Dock, and can toggle on/off the annoy-ing little bouncing that occurs when you launch an application. You have the option of keeping the Dock visible at all times, or having it hidden, only appearing when your cursor moves over the area where the Dock would normally be. As for the stuff that used to be in the Apple Menu options for Mac OS 9, there are no submenu controls—if you want to see a list of what's in a folder in the Dock, just Control-click on it.

Adding Items to the Apple Menu OS 9

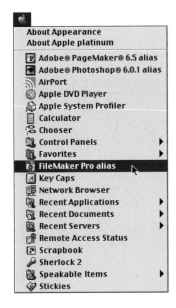

OS 9: Back in OS 9, to add an application to the Apple menu (for convenient launching) you'd start by locating the application file, then click on it and press Command-M to make an alias. Then you'd open the System Folder, find the Apple Menu Items folder, then drop the alias in there, and that alias would be added to the Apple menu. Sounds kind of like a pain, and it was.

Adding Items to [now called] the Dock OS X

Divider

Applications

All other items

A triangle under an Icon indicates that the application is open.

OS X: In Mac OS X, not only can you put just about anything in the Dock for quick access— it is incredibly easy to do. To put an application in the Dock, locate it on your drive and drag its icon to the Dock. Mac OS X automatically makes an alias which stays in the Dock. You can do the same with folders, individual documents, songs—anything you want. Do you connect to a server every day? Drag it to the Dock. Web site? No problem. Click on the URL in your Web browser and drag it to the Dock. It's a beautiful thing. There is one rule: Only applications can be placed to the left of the Dock's divider line. Any other type of file must go to the right. If you try to put something where it doesn't belong (and I know you will because you're a Mac user), it won't work.

new stuff:	*Now, when you launch an application, its icon temporarily appears in the Dock. If you want to keep an alias of this application in the Dock (for easy one-click launching), just Control-click on the application's Dock icon and choose Keep in Dock from the pop-up menu.*	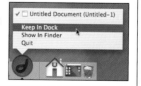

Launching the Apple System Profiler OS 9

OS 9: To launch the Apple System Profiler back in Mac OS 9, you'd go under the Apple menu and choose Apple System Profiler. This would launch the utility and present a complete profile of your system software and hardware (particularly helpful to Apple service techs, who'll ask for info from this utility if you ever have a problem that requires service).

Launching the Apple System Profiler OS X

OS X: Now, you can access the Apple System Profiler by going under the Apple menu and choosing About this Computer. When the About window appears, click on the button for More Info to launch the Apple System Profiler (it doesn't say that pressing that button will launch the Apple System Profiler, but it does—freaky, I know).

new stuff: *Above, I showed the easiest way to access the Apple System Profiler, but if you were in the mood to dig around instead, it's actually found within the Utilities folder, which is within the Applications folder.*

Accessing the Calculator OS 9

OS 9: Apple's age-old calculator (I call it "age-old" because it has looked exactly the same for as long as I've used a Mac) is found under the Apple menu in OS 9. Just choose Calculator, and up comes that tiny awful-looking gray and black calculator shown above. However, if you went to your Utilities folder and opened the Graphing Calculator, you were in for a treat. I would put that baby in demo mode and watch it create beautiful shapes for hours. The main problem with the Graphing Calculator was that you had to have an I.Q. high enough to boil water in order to use it, which probably explains why it was left out of Mac OS X.

Accessing the Calculator OS X

OS X: There's good news and bad news. First the good news: At long last, Apple has updated the look of the calculator: They made it bigger, cooler looking, and they've added more functionality. The bad news: Now that Apple has improved it to the point that you might actually use it, they hid it. You'd think it would appear in the Dock by default (especially since the calculator has lived in the Apple menu for years) but no, that would be too easy. Instead, they tossed it in the Applications folder along with all the other goodies. Go to your Applications folder and you'll find it hiding there (it's still named, simply, Calculator). Once it's open, if you want to keep it in your Dock for quicker access, just Control-click on its Dock icon and choose Keep in Dock from the pop-up menu that appears.

new stuff:	*If you've got a big über-brain for math, click on the Advanced button to reveal the added functionality of the OS X calculator.* Note: *if you find yourself using the advanced mode often, it might explain why you didn't have a date for the prom.*	

Accessing the Chooser (for Printing) OS 9

OS 9: Back in OS 9, before you could print a document, you'd have to go to the Chooser and tell your Mac which printer you wanted to use. If you had only one printer, you only had to do this once, and then your Mac would remember it next time. But if you had multiple printers, you'd wind up in the Chooser fairly often. To use the Chooser you went to the Apple menu and selected Chooser. In the Chooser window a list of print drivers appeared in the left column. When you clicked on one, a list of connected printers that used that driver appeared in the right window. You selected the one you wanted to use and closed the Chooser. If you ever wanted to print to a different printer, you had to go through this process again. Like I said, if you had multiple printers you got pretty good at using the Chooser.

[Now Called] Print Center OS X

OS X: There is no Chooser in Mac OS X. To select printer options you now go to Print Center (a name which, frankly, makes much more sense to new users). Print Center is found inside your Applications folder, within the Utilities folder (as shown above left). If you launch Print Center, a list of printers connected to your Mac (or to your network) will appear, and you can choose which printer you want to use simply by clicking on it in the list of available printers. Since Print Center is an application, it appears in the Dock whenever you print. For convenience, you might want to Control-click on its Dock icon and select Keep in Dock from the pop-up menu.

new stuff: *Print Center makes using multiple printers easy. Every time you tell a document to print you have the ability to select a different printer right from the print dialog. If the one you want isn't listed, there is an option to edit your printer list. This launches Print Center (not having to hunt for it) and lets you select the printer you want to add to your list of active printers.*

Accessing Control Panels OS 9

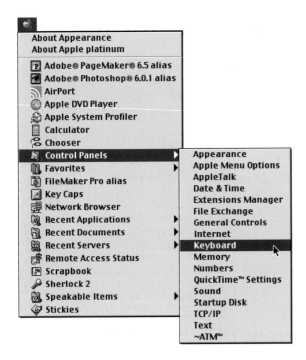

OS 9: Back in Mac OS 9, the fastest way to get to get to the System's Control Panels was to go under the Apple Menu to Control Panels. If you paused for a second, a hierarchical menu opened (as shown above) and you could choose a Control Panel to open.

[Now Called] System Preferences OS X

OS X: In Mac OS X, Control Panels have have been replaced by System Preferences (shown above). To access them, go to the Apple menu and choose System Preferences. Click on any individual item in System Preferences to reveal its Preference pane. By default, the Preferences are arranged by category. If you would rather see them arranged alphabetically, from the menu bar select View and choose Show All Alphabetically from the drop-down menu.

new stuff:	*After you open System Preferences, make a change, and close the System Preferences window, it doesn't actually quit. That's right. System Preferences is really an application and, unless you choose Quit or press Command-Q, it stays active and in the Dock, even though its window is hidden from view. That's actually pretty handy—if you want these preferences back in a hurry, just click on the System Preferences icon in the Dock.*

Creating and Accessing Favorites OS 9

OS 9: In Mac OS 9 when you wanted to add a document or folder to your Favorites, you clicked once on its icon then went to the menu bar and selected File. From the drop-down menu you then selected Add to Favorites. Of course, if you didn't need to impress the person looking over your shoulder by making something simple look like rocket science, you could always just click on the document's icon and press Command-T. Not very impressive, but fast. To access your Favorites, you'd just go under the Apple menu, look in the Favorites folder, and it would be there.

Creating and Accessing Favorites OS X

OS X: When you want to add an item to your Favorites in Mac OS X just locate its icon and drag it onto the Favorites button (the big red heart) that is, by default, on the toolbar of every Finder window. To access your Favorites, choose Go from the Finder's menu bar and scroll down to Favorites in the drop-down menu that opens.

new stuff: *When you're saving documents, you now also have quick access to your list of Favorites (which makes saving to your most-used folders quick and easy) as most OS X-native applications list your Favorites in their Save As dialog (in the Where pop-up menu, as shown at right). This enables you to easily save a document right to one of your Favorites without having to go digging through your drive.*

Accessing Key Caps OS 9

OS 9: Back in OS 9, to access Key Caps (the utility that let you find the keyboard locations for hidden font characters, like ©, ™, and é) you'd go under the Apple menu and choose Key Caps. That brought up the Key Caps utility (shown above right) which looks like a tiny keyboard. Once open, you could hold the Option or Shift key (or both) and the mini-keyboard would then display the characters that would appear if you typed a letter with that modifier key held down. For example, if you held the Option key down and looked at the Key Caps keyboard, you'd see that the letter G now displayed the © symbol. So then you'd know that pressing Option-G on your real keyboard would give the copyright symbol (©).

Accessing Key Caps OS X

OS X: Now, Key Caps is found in the Utilities folder inside the Applications folder (above left). Double-click it to launch Key Caps, which looks and works pretty much like the original Key Caps, just with a fresh coat of Aqua paint. But here's something new: Click the green Zoom button on the Key Caps title bar and you get a bigger keyboard.

new stuff:	There's another way to find hidden characters in some OS X-native applications. If the application uses Mac OS X's built-in Fonts palette (like TextEdit for example), open that panel, then from the Extras pop-up menu at the bottom of the Font panel, choose Show Characters. This brings up the Character palette (shown at right) where you can easily find hidden characters by choosing a category from the left column, which displays character choices in the right column. If you find a hidden character you'll want to use again, click the Add to Favorites button, then you can click the Favorites tab and insert that hidden character into your document by pressing the Insert button.

Accessing Recently Used Items OS 9

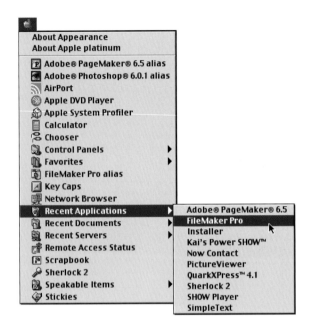

OS 9: Back in Mac OS 9, there were two folders in the Apple menu that gave you convenient access to the files and applications you most recently used. To access these, you'd
just go under the Apple menu, to the folder named Recent Applications or Recent Documents and choose the recently used application or file you want to open.

Accessing Recently Used Items OS X

OS X: Now there's just one menu item for accessing both recently used applications and documents. Go under the Apple menu and choose Recent Items. A hierarchical menu will open listing Recent Applications first, followed by Recent Documents. Just scroll to the item you want to open and click once to open it.

new stuff:	In Mac OS X, Apple has added a new command which you will find at the bottom of the Recent Items list. It's called Clear Menu and it does exactly what is says— clears the list of both recently used Applications and Documents. So when you're finished playing Quake, select Clear Menus and launch Photoshop, InDesign and Word. The next person to use your Mac will be very impressed.

Chapter Two

 One of the things that Apple didn't change "a whole bunch" (that's a technical term) is how windows, icons, and stuff (another technical term) work in Mac OS X. Oh don't you worry, they moved just enough stuff around to make you feel

Windows, Icons, and Stuff
DOES THIS REALLY NEED A DESCRIPTION?

ill-at-ease for a few days, but not enough that you'll think you're using Windows XP. This chapter (dedicated to authors everywhere who, when faced with the problem of coming up with a word to describe certain elements of a computer operating system, rather than going through the time-consuming research route, opted instead to use the word "stuff") looks at how these things have changed, from the subtle nuances to the—the—ah heck, they're all subtle nuances, but they're not so subtle that you wouldn't notice; yet they're subtle enough to subtly remind you that things have changed. I'm rambling again, aren't I? Look, here's what it comes down to—I couldn't come up with anything particularly clever to say about windows, icons and stuff, and frankly, If I hadn't used the word "stuff" in the title, and found a way to work the word "subtle" into this chapter intro several times, this would be just a couple of lines, and then my editor would have insisted that I write more. Now, because I know for a fact that editors don't read chapter intros—they just look to see that a reasonable amount of text is there, that I could get away with this rambling. Perhaps even random words. Let's see: Fishbarn cement cow seaweed dander. See, they never check this stuff. *[Oh, yes they do! And it isn't easy. —Ed.]*

Changing Window Views OS 9

OS 9: Back in Mac OS 9 you had your choice of three views: Icon view, List view, and the always popular (among the eight people who actually used it) but seldom used big ugly Button view. The default was Icon view, but if you wanted to switch to one of the others, you would just choose As List or As Buttons from the View menu on the Finder's menu bar.

Changing Window Views OS X

OS X: In Mac OS X you still have three choices: Icon view, List view, and the new and wonderful Column view. At the top of every Finder window is a toolbar. Toward the left end of the toolbar you will see the three View buttons (circled above). The first (from the left) is for viewing your window contents by icon. The second (middle button) is for List view, and click the third for the new Column view. *Note:* if the toolbar is not visible, just click the clear pill-shaped button at the top far right side of the title bar.

new stuff:	*The Column view is new to Macintosh, and many people like it so much it's the only view they use, because they claim they can get to where they want faster by moving left to right, rather than digging through folders.*

Opening Folders in a New Window OS 9

OS 9: In Mac OS 9, you really didn't have a choice about this; any time you opened a folder, it opened its own separate window. This made for a lot of open windows (which tended to clutter your desktop), but it made copying files from one window to another pretty effortless.

Opening Folders in a New Window OS X

OS X: Now, in Mac OS X, by default when you open a folder it doesn't open a new window. Instead, the contents of the folder replace the contents of the current window (much like a Web browser, where you click on a link, and the new Web page appears in place of the old Web page). To have a folder open in its own separate window, now you hold the Command key before you open the folder.

new stuff:	*If you hold the Option key when clicking on a folder, it not only opens the folder in its own separate window, but also immediately closes the original window where the folder resided.*

Tidying Up Windows (Snap to Grid) OS 9

OS 9: In Mac OS 9, to have the icons in your open window snap to an invisible grid (handy for housekeeping purposes), you'd go under the View menu located on the Finder's menu bar and choose View Options (the shortcut was Command-J). The dialog pictured above presented you with several options for arranging the items on your desktop that you could set to your liking. The next time your desktop was a mess, all you had to do was click on the view menu and choose Clean Up and your desktop was instantly neat and organized.

Tidying Up Windows (Snap to Grid) OS X

OS X: Now, to have the icons in your window (if you are in Icon view) snap to an invisible grid, press Command-J to bring up the View Preferences dialog (above right), then turn on the checkbox for Snap to grid. The name of the command might lead you to believe that your icons will instantly snap to the grid—they don't. If you're getting paid by the hour, grab each icon individually and drag them a bit. When you let go they'll snap into place. Otherwise, select View from the Menu bar then choose Clean Up from the pull-down menu. Now all your icons will line up to the grid at once.

new stuff:	You have the option of turning on this option for just the open, active window or for all windows by checking the boxes in the View Preferences dialog. When you turn on Snap to grid, you'll see a tiny icon of a grid in the left-hand corner of your window's Info bar (directly below the title bar).	

Collapsing a Window OS 9

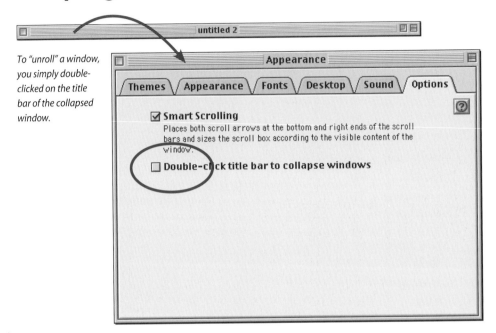

To "unroll" a window, you simply double-clicked on the title bar of the collapsed window.

OS 9: In Mac OS 9 you could double-click on a window's title bar, and it would "roll up" like a window shade, leaving only the window's title bar still visible. To turn on this function, you'd go under the Apple Menu, into the Control Panels folder and choose Appearance. In the Appearance folder, you'd click on the Options tab and turn on the checkbox labeled Double-click title bar to collapse windows.

Collapsing a Window OS X

OS X: Windowshading is no longer available in Mac OS X but it's been replaced by some-thing better—minimizing to the Dock. In the top left corner of every window there are three round buttons. (If you've kept the default Blue option in the Appearance preference pane they're red, yellow, and green. If you've chosen the Graphite option they're all gray.) When you want to clear a window from the desktop but want to be able to retrieve it quickly, click the yellow (or middle) button and the window will shrink down to the Dock (technically this is called "minimizing"). When you want it back, click on its dock image.

new stuff:	Start playing a QuickTime movie. While it's playing, click the yellow button to minimize it. Look at its image in the Dock. Yep, still playing! When you minimize a document's window it remains active. Besides being cool, it's useful. If you are rendering an iMovie project, for instance, a quick glance at the Dock will let you know if it's done or still rendering.

Closing a Window OS 9

OS 9: To close a window in Mac OS 9, you'd click on the Close box in its upper left-hand corner. You could also press Command-W as a shortcut (if you're too lazy to click. Like me).

Closing a Window OS X

OS X: I know this one may seem a little "duh" but I've had people who've just switched to Mac OS X ask this one. They weren't the sharpest people mind you, but they did ask. Now, to close a window, you click on the red close button at the top far left, and you can still use the old Command-W shortcut to close the window via keyboard. Again, if you're charging by the hour, you could go under the Finder menu and choose Close Window, but as far as I can tell, that has actually only been used once in the history of Mac OS X, and then only by someone whose keyboard and mouse were both irreparably damaged, and they could only navigate by using the arrow keys on the keyboard; and even at that, they might have been lying. *Note:* Clicking the red close button closes the window, but does not quit the associated application. The application's icon remains in the Dock and you will notice the triangle below it indicating that it is still running.

Closing All Open Windows OS 9

OS 9: In Mac OS 9, to quickly close every open window for a single application you could Option-click on the close box in the upper left corner of any open window, and all open windows for the same application would close.

Closing All Open Windows OS X

OS X: Now, you do pretty much the same thing—you Option-click on the red close button in the upper left-hand corner of the title bar and all open windows for that application will close. You haven't quit the application, just closed all its windows. Here's a couple more shortcuts that are handy when working with multiple windows. If you are working with several applications and want to see only the windows for one of them, Option-Command-click on the application's Dock icon. Any open windows for other applications will be hidden. The beauty is, they're not closed. Click on their applications' Dock icons and they will be visible again. Option-clicking on the Dock icon of the active application will hide its windows. Option-click on it again and they're back.

new stuff:	*Want to minimize all the open windows for a particular application to the Dock? Option-click on the yellow (middle) button of one of them and they will all get sucked down to the Dock until you need them again.*

Zoom Your Window OS 9

OS 9: Why is it that the picture you need to see or the information you need to copy off the screen is always covered up by a window that takes up half your screen? In Mac OS 9 if you wanted to instantly make a window smaller (or larger) all you had to do was go to the upper right-hand corner of its title bar, locate the two little square boxes and click on the one on the left. I always called it "That little box in the top right-hand corner of the window," but for the geeks among you who like to use the technical terms for things, it is officially known as the Zoom Box. If your window is big, it zooms it small. If it's small, it zooms it big.

Zoom Your Window OS X

OS X: Now in Mac OS X, to zoom an open window you click on the green zoom button (the third button from the left) at the upper left-hand corner of your window's title bar. This button seems kind of lame, but it may save you someday. In Mac OS X you can only move windows by grabbing them at the top or bottom. Every now and then you will get a window that somehow gets bigger than your screen (I suspect it's steroids, but I've never been able to prove it) and you can't see the top or bottom. When this happens, just click the green button and your window will shrink until it fits on your screen again, allowing you to move it or resize it.

new stuff:	*Just in case you forget which little window button does what, if you put your cursor over any one of the buttons, they'll give you a hint. As you roll over them, an "X" appears over the red button (letting you know that this closes the window); a minus sign appears over the yellow button (letting you know that clicking it will minimize the window), and a plus (+) sign appears over the green button, letting you know that clicking on it will maximize (zoom) the window.*

Making a New Folder OS 9

OS 9: In Mac OS 9 there were two ways to make a new folder. The first was to go to the File menu and select New Folder. Now, actually choosing this from the menu (rather than using the keyboard shortcut) is only for the wimpiest, scaredy-cat, big-baby, wuss-head, Mac user (not you of course, but surely you can think of a friend that fits that description). The power user (you, for example) would press Command-N to create a new folder. Simple. Easy. Elegant. It was actually the perfect keyboard shortcut. That's probably why Apple decided to change it in Mac OS X.

Making a New Folder OS X

OS X: Now, you press Shift-Command-N (I know, I know, how could they change this particular keyboard shortcut after all these years?), or you can simply Control-click on any open space within a Finder window (or on the Desktop), and a pop-up menu will appear allowing you to choose New Folder (as shown above). I prefer this method, partially as my own personal protest against using Shift-Command-N.

Changing Folder/File Names OS 9

Old Name

Old Name Selected

New Name

OS 9: To change a folder name in Mac OS 9, the easiest way was either to click on the file *name* you wanted to change, or to click on the *icon* of the file and then press the Return key. Either action would highlight the name of the file for you, so all you had to do was type in a new name.

Changing Folder/File Names OS X

OS X: Now, when in either Icon or List view, or on the Desktop, you can click directly on a file's name and it highlights, ready for you to type in a new name. In Column view, you click on a icon, then press the Return key to highlight it; but honestly—except in Column view—since you can click directly on the name and it highlights, why would you want to click, then press Return? It's just extra work—back-breaking work (if you will) and totally unnecessary.

new stuff:	*If you're charging by the hour, there's another way to change a file's name. Click on the file's icon, then press Command-I to bring up the file's Info window. Then, in the File Info window, choose Name and Extension. This will bring up a field where you can name the file.*	

43

Color Coding Folders/Files OS 9

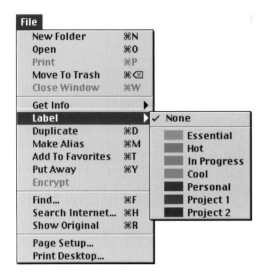

OS 9: Back in Mac OS 9, you could color code files by clicking on the icon of a file or folder, then you'd go under the File menu, under Label, and assign a color (as shown above).

Color Coding Folders/Files OS X

Go to the Info window, to the Comment field, and add your comments.

To view the Comments field (when in List view), go to the View Preferences, then under Show Columns, turn on Comments.

You can now view these comments when in List view.

OS X: Apple has replaced color coding with the ability to add comments to your files which can be viewed in any window set to List View. To add a comment, click on the file, then press Command-I to bring up the file's Info window. At the bottom of the Info window is the Comments pane. Click on the disclosure triangle (right-facing arrow) before the word Comments to make that field visible, then enter your comments (as shown, top left). Then, to see a file's comments, you have to "turn them on" for the window containing that file. Open a window, press Command-J to bring up the View Preferences (as shown top right), and turn on the checkbox for Comments (as shown). Now, for every file in that window the Comments field will be visible (as shown at bottom, above). By default, the Comments column appears at the far right.

Docking a Folder to the Bottom of Your Screen OS 9

OS 9: Back in OS 9, once a window was open in the Finder, you could click on the title bar and drag it to the bottom of the screen, and it would stay there, with just a small tab sticking up. When you wanted to pop open that window again, you'd just click on the tab and it would appear on screen.

Minimizing a Folder to the Dock OS X

OS X: Now, you can add a folder or file to the bottom of your screen by minimizing it to the Dock. You do this by either clicking once on the yellow (center) button on the top left of any window (as shown at top), or by just pressing Command-M while the window is active. Then to access the window again (have it pop up on screen), just click on it once in the Dock (as shown above). To let you know that a Dock icon is actually a minimized window a tiny icon of the application that created the window is added to the lower right-hand corner of its Dock image. It's easily visible when viewed in the Dock, as you can see in the lower capture of the two shown above.

| new stuff: | *If you want to turn off the Genie effect that you see when you put items in the Dock, Control-click on the Dock's divider line. When the pop-up menu appears, select Minimize using Scale Effect.* | |

Making Aliases of Files or Folders OS 9

OS 9: Back in Mac OS 9, you'd click on the file that you wanted to make an alias of, then you'd press Command-M. You could also hold Option-Command while you dragged the folder or file for which you wanted to make an alias.

Making Aliases of Files or Folders OS X

OS X: Now, you click on the file for which you want an alias, then you press Command-L (the shortcut changed because the old Command-M shortcut is now used to minimize a window to the Dock). So why did I show the menu command above? Just to tease you. If you're not getting paid by the hour, here's a quicker way to make an alias. Hold down the Option and Command keys while you drag the file you want to make an alias of right out of the window it appears in. Instant alias. Drag it to either the Desktop or another window or folder. It may not really be faster, but it's great for making lesser Mac users feel, well…lesser.

Find the Original for an Alias OS 9

OS 9: Aliases are great—so great that you can accumulate hundreds of them on your hard drive and forget where the original files are saved. Back in Mac OS 9, when you needed to find the original file for an alias you Control-clicked on the alias and chose Show Original from the contextual menu that opened.

Find the Original for an Alias OS X

File

New Finder Window	⌘N
New Folder	⇧⌘N
Open	⌘O
Open With	▶
Close Window	⌘W
Get Info	⌘I
Duplicate	⌘D
Make Alias	⌘L
Show Original	⌘R
Add to Favorites	⌘T
Move to Trash	⌘⌫
Eject	⌘E
Burn Disc...	
Find...	⌘F

Meg's ideas.fp5
alias

OS X: Unfortunately upgrading to Mac OS X doesn't do a thing to improve your memory. No problem—this function works the same as it did in Mac OS 9. Control-click on an alias and choose Show Original from the pop-up menu. If you prefer, you can also click once on the alias to highlight it then go to the File menu and choose Show Original (shown above).

Finding Files on Your Mac OS 9

OS 9: In Mac OS 9, to find a particular file on your Mac, you'd press Command-F to bring up Sherlock 2 (shown above), enter the file's name (or other attribute) into Sherlock's Find field, then press the Magnifying Glass button to the right of the Find field to start your search.

Finding Files on Your Mac OS X

OS X: In Mac OS X, you still use Command-F, but it now opens the window shown above (Sherlock is now only used for Internet searches). You can refine your search by using the "Search in" and "Add criteria" pop-up menus available in the search window. An additional search feature in Mac OS X is a search entry window built into the toolbar of every Finder window. Just highlight the folder(s) you want to search, type in the name of the file you're trying to find, and press the Enter or Return key.

new stuff:	*Mac OS X (and many applications) install huge amounts of language support—some for languages I'm not sure are even spoken. Besides taking up space on your hard drive, they slow up things like searching because your Mac looks through all those files every time you do a search. Here's how to speed things up. From the Finder, go to the menu bar, select Finder and choose Preferences. Click on the Select button at the bottom of the box that opens and you can select only the language(s) you want included in searches.*

Deleting Files OS 9

OS 9: To Delete a file in Mac OS 9, you'd drag it to the Trash icon at the bottom right-hand corner of your Desktop (or wherever you kept it). The file was not actually deleted at this point—just sitting in the trash. If you changed your mind you could take it back out again. To delete the file, you had to choose Empty Trash from the Special menu (or Option-click on the Trash icon and select Empty Trash from the pop-up menu).

Deleting Files OS X

Finder

About Finder	
Preferences...	
Empty Trash	⇧⌘⌫
Services	▶
Hide Finder	⌘H
Hide Others	⌥⌘H
Show All	

Since Mac OS X is designed to run in a multi-user environment, each user has their own trash can which other users can't access. If you fill your trash then log out it will still be waiting for you the next time you log in. It doesn't matter how many other people have logged in or whether they have emptied the trash—your trash is still safe.

Empty Trash

OS X: In Mac OS X, it's pretty much the same. You have to start by putting the file you want to delete in the Trash, but the trash can has moved. It's no longer in the bottom right-hand corner of your Desktop. Instead, it's at the far right of the Dock (although a faster method of "trashing" a file is to just click on the file, then press Command-Delete. This places the file into the Trash for you lickety-split). Then, to actually delete the file and any others that are in the trash, now you go under the File menu (rather than the Special menu, which no longer exists) and choose Empty Trash (or use the Empty Trash keyboard shortcut: Shift-Command-Delete).

new stuff:	*You can combine the two shortcuts above to create an über shortcut which not only puts your file in the trash for you, but also empties the trash upon its arrival. Perfect for any file so vile that you can't bear to have it on your drive a moment longer. Just click on the file you want "outta here," then press Command-Delete, then Shift-Command-Delete. That puppy is now gone for good!*

Chapter Three

You may find it hard to believe, but people are different. (This came as somewhat a shock to me. I always assumed everybody was like me.) However, once you think about it,

Customizing Your Mac
SETTING UP YOUR SYSTEM TO YOUR TASTE

it explains a lot of things (like the Anna Nicole show and Monster Truck and Tractor pulls—not everyone thinks those are cool as I do, which I found disconcerting, to say the least). So it's entirely possible that once you start working with Mac OS X, you might be tempted to change some of the system preferences to suit your own tastes, needs, and work habits. Here's the thing: Don't do it. Why? Because only I am allowed to change the defaults. You see, as I mentioned earlier, people are different, and they basically fall into two categories: (1) You, and (2) Me. Through a special arrangement with Apple's executive management, only I am allowed to change the user preferences of Mac OS X, because I am, after all, the different one. However, should you be feeling a bit "me-ish" and want a glimpse into what it's like being "me" (without all the limos, parties with Puffy, flowing Cristal, and paparazzi, of course), then turn the page to learn how to make your Mac, your way. You're so "me."

Setting the Date & Time OS 9

OS 9: Back in OS 9, to change the time or date, you'd go under the Apple menu, to the Control Panels folder, and choose Date & Time. You would set the time by highlighting the time fields and typing in the date and time (or by using the up/down arrow buttons).

Setting the Date & Time OS X

OS X: Now to set the Date & Time you go under the Apple menu and choose System Prefer-ences. When the System Preferences pane appears, click on the Date & Time icon which brings up the pane shown above. Set Today's Date by clicking on the appropriate adjust-ment arrows. To set the time, click directly on the hour, minute, or seconds field you want to adjust and click the up or down arrow as appropriate. You can type a number directly into any field instead of using the arrows. Note that if you have selected Use a Network Time Server in the Network Time tab, the adjustment arrows won't appear. The date and time will be set automatically when you go online. *Geek tip:* You can actually set the time by dragging the hands of the clock. Is this an efficient way to set the time? Hardly. But does it make you look cool? Oh yeah.

new stuff:	You can also quickly get to the Date & Time preference pane by clicking and holding on the clock that appears in your menu bar (at the top right corner of your screen). When the drop-down menu appears, choose Open Date & Time. It doesn't get much quicker than that.

Setting the Number of Recent Apps OS 9

OS 9: Your Mac keeps track of the last applications and documents you opened. This is pretty handy, because many people wind up working in the same few applications, and often on the same document, over and over again. By remembering these recently used applications and documents, you can quickly jump right to the file you need, without having to dig around your hard drive, searching through folders, etc. Instead, if you want to open a recently used application, you go under the Apple menu, click and hold on the Recent applications folder, and a list of your most recently used apps appears. It works the same way for documents. However, you get to decide just how many apps and documents your Mac keeps track of. Back in OS 9, you'd set the number of recently opened applications and documents by going under the Apple menu, to the Control Panels folder, and choosing Apple Menu Options. The somewhat cheesy-looking dialog above would appear, where you could type in the number of items you wanted your Mac to keep track of.

Setting the Number of Recent Apps OS X

OS X: Now, you go under the Apple menu and choose System Preferences. Click on the General Preferences icon to bring up the General Preferences pane, and in the section for Recent Items, click on the pop-up menu (there's one for Applications and for Documents). Choose the number of recently used items you want your Mac to make available from the Apple menu's Recent Items menu. Now, when you go under the Apple menu and choose Recent Items, the list will display the number of recently used applications and documents you chose in the preferences pane.

new stuff:	*When you use the Recent Items feature (not the preferences shown above, the actual feature found under the Apple menu), at the very bottom of the list is something new—the menu command Clear list which does just that—it clears all of the recent applications or documents, and starts over.*

Changing the Highlight Color OS 9

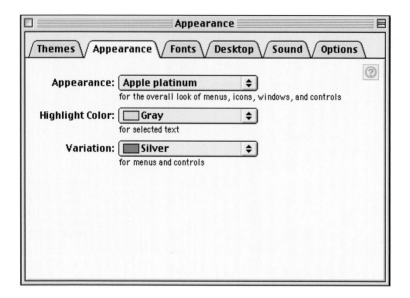

OS 9: When you click on an icon, the name of the file highlights in color (to let you know it's selected). You can change the color of this highlighting (and I always did) to any color you'd like. (I usually choose a vivid yellow, but hey, that's just me.) Back in Mac OS 9, to change the Highlight Color you'd go under the Apple menu, to the Control Panels folder, and choose Appearance. The dialog shown above would appear and you could select your desired color from the Highlight Color pop-up menu.

Changing the Highlight Color OS X

OS X: Now you choose your Highlight Color from the General Preferences pane. Go under the Apple menu and choose System Preferences. When the Preferences pane appears, click on the General Preferences icon to bring up its Preference pane. Near the top of the pane is the Highlight Color pop-up menu. Choose your Highlight Color from the preset colors shown here, or choose Other to pick your own custom Highlight color from a pop-up color picker that will appear.

Adjusting Overall Volume OS 9

OS 9: Back in Mac OS 9 to adjust the overall volume of your Mac, you'd go under the Apple menu, to the Control Panels folder, and choose Sound. When the Sound dialog appeared, you'd click on the Output tab (as shown above) to bring up the Output panel. At the bottom of this panel is a slider that you'd use to adjust the volume or to Mute the output volume entirely.

Adjusting Overall Volume OS X

OS X: Now to adjust the overall volume of your Mac you click on the Apple menu and choose System Preferences. When the dialog appears, click on the Sound icon to bring up the Sound Preferences pane. It doesn't matter which tab you choose here, because the Output volume slider appears at the bottom of all of them. (How's that for convenient?)

new stuff:	*Want the ultimate in speed? The next time you have the Sound Preference pane open, click on the checkbox for Show volume in menu bar. Now you can access the Output volume slider right from the menu bar at the top right of your screen. You'll see a little black icon of a speaker—click once on it and a volume slider will drop down (as shown at right). How cool is that!*

Changing the System Font Size OS 9

OS 9: If you're using a high resolution monitor setting (and most new Macs' native screen resolution is so high that it makes your icons look miniature) chances are the text on screen is pretty darn small (like the text below icons, in lists, etc.). Back in Mac OS 9 you could change the size of your Views font by going under the Apple menu and in the Control Panels folder choosing Appearance. In the Appearance dialog, click on the Fonts tab, and there's a field for choosing your Views Font size (it's circled above).

Changing the System Font Size OS X

OS X: Now, you can choose the font size you'd like for any individual window (giving you the choice of having the text larger in some windows, smaller in others. It's the ultimate in font size personalization). Just open the Finder Window where you'd like to change the font size, then press Command-J (or click on View in the Menu bar and choose View Options). When the View preferences pane opens you'll see a pop-up menu with preset Text sizes for you to choose from (as shown above). If you want to affect just this one window, choose This Window Only at the top of the View Preferences dialog. If you want to change sizes system-wide and haven't set any other windows to This Window Only, choose All Windows.

new stuff: *Back in Mac OS 9, Apple let you easily change the System font, as well as the size, but in OS X you can only change the size. Why? Because they're evil, evil I tell you! (Which really means, I don't know, but it sounds much better than "I don't know.")*

Choosing Scroll Bar Arrows OS 9

OS 9: By default, in any window that has scroll bars, the little scroll arrows (the ones you click to scroll up and down) are located at the top and bottom of the side scroll bar, and the far left and right of the bottom scroll bar. However, some people think it's more convenient to have both the up/down and left/right scroll arrows appear together, at the bottom right corner of the active window. These people are freaks (just kidding). In Mac OS 9, this feature was called Smart Scrolling. (Only to make these freaks feel better about themselves. Again, just a joke. Sort of.) To turn on Smart Scrolling, you went under the Apple menu and in the Control Panels folder chose Appearance. When the Appearance Preference panel appeared you clicked on the Options Tab (the far right one) and then on the checkbox for Smart Scrolling. This placed the scroll arrows together at the bottom right corner of the window. It also automatically made the scroll box (that little box you drag around in the scroll bar) shrink and grow based on what proportion of the window was visible.

Choosing Scroll Bar Arrows OS X

OS X: Now you turn this feature on/off by going under the Apple menu and choosing System Preferences. Click on the General Preferences icon. The middle section has a Place scroll arrows option. Choose Together by clicking its radio button. In Mac OS X the resizing of the scroller, or "thumb," is always on, regardless of which scroll arrow option you choose.

Changing Your Desktop Background OS 9

OS 9: To change the Desktop background pattern, you'd go under the Apple menu, under Control Panels, and choose Appearance. When the Appearance dialog appeared, you'd click on the Desktop tab and then you could choose one of the lame, I mean built-in desktop patterns. There was also a button called Place Picture which let you choose a photo for your desktop background. Once you had the pattern or photo you wanted in the Preview Window, to apply it as your desktop you had to press the Set Desktop button at the bottom right of the dialog.

Changing Your Desktop Background OS X

OS X: Now you go under the Apple menu and choose System Preferences. When the Preference pane appears, click on Desktop to bring up the Desktop Preference pane (shown above). A pop-up menu lets you choose from different collections of background images. To choose a desktop, just click on it from the scrolling list. That's all there is to it. If you want to add one of your own images to the list, just drag and drop it straight into the large preview window at the top left of the pane. Incidentally, there's no Set Desktop button like in the old days. Now, when you click on a pattern it becomes your desktop until you choose a different one.

new stuff:	In Mac OS X, there's now a Change Picture option, and you can choose to have the system automatically choose a new desktop at different time intervals, when your computer wakes from sleep, or when logging in. There's a Random order checkbox (as shown above) to have your Mac choose a random desktop background each time; otherwise it will display each new background in the order they appear in the scroll box.

Choosing Your Numbers Format OS 9

OS 9: You have the option of setting how your numbers are presented, based on which country you live in. For example, you'd choose which symbol is used to denote money, like $ or £, and whether the symbol goes before the number (like $1,500) or after it (like 1,500£). Back in OS 9, these were set by going under the Apple menu, inside the Control Panels folder, and choosing Numbers. This brought up the Numbers dialog, where you could choose the number format from the pop-up menu at the top of the dialog, or type your choices manually in the fields. A sample of how your symbols will appear was at the bottom of the dialog.

Choosing Your Numbers Format OS X

OS X: Now, the Numbers format is in an entirely different location. Go under the Apple menu and choose System Preferences. In the System Preferences pane, click on the International icon . When the International Preference pane appears, click on the Numbers tab and the pane shown above will appear. Choose your region from the pop-up menu, or manually enter your choices in the fields if your region is not in the list.

new stuff: *New in the OS X version of the Numbers Preferences pane is the option of choosing the Metric system as your unit of measurement. Frasier and Niles would definitely choose this option, and they'd probably choose France as their region, even though they live in Seattle.*

Adjusting Your Mouse/Trackpad Speed OS 9

OS 9: You could control the speed of your mouse (for desktop machines) or your PowerBook/ iBook trackpad through a control panel. You'd go under the Apple menu, under Control Panels, and choose Mouse (for desktop Macs) or Trackpad (for PowerBooks/iBooks).

Adjusting Your Mouse/Trackpad Speed OS X

OS X: Now we adjust either the Mouse speed (for desktop Macs) or Trackpad speed (for PowerBooks/iBooks) in the same place. From the Apple menu, open System Preferences and click on the Mouse icon to bring up the Mouse Preference pane (as shown above). Here you can choose the Tracking Speed (how fast your mouse moves around the screen), the speed you want your Mac to recognize that two clicks is a "double-click," and at the bottom of the pane are options for using the trackpad on your PowerBook.

Setting Your Keyboard Layout OS 9

OS 9: You set the keyboard layout (depending on which language you use) by going under the Apple menu, under Control Panels, and choosing Keyboard. This brought up the dialog shown above, where you'd choose your country, and this would map the keyboard of your Mac appropriately. This was always a great starting point for pulling pranks on other people in your office while they were out at lunch.

Setting your Keyboard Layout OS X

OS X: Now, the keyboard layout isn't part of Keyboard System Preferences at all. Instead, from the Apple menu choose System Preferences and click on the International icon. Click on the tab for Input Menu (as shown above) to bring up the list of international keyboard layouts.

Open Applications Automatically at Startup OS 9

OS 9: To have a program launch automatically upon startup, you would click on its icon and make an alias of that file. Then you'd open the System folder, find a folder named Startup Items, and place the alias there. From the next restart onward, that program (and any others with aliases in the folder) would launch automatically.

Open Applications Automatically at Startup OS X

OS X: Now you don't have to mess with aliases and dropping things in the System folder anymore. You just go under the Apple menu and choose System Preferences. Click on the icon for Login Items to bring up the Login Items Preference pane (shown above). Click the Add button and navigate to the application you want to launch upon login. You can use this method to add as many applications as you'd like.

new stuff:	If you have several applications set to open automatically, your screen can easily get covered with open windows which you'll have to close. If you would like an item to launch at startup but remain in the background, select the checkbox next to its name in the Login Items Preference pane. You'll know the application is open from its Dock icon, but it won't clutter your desktop.

Adjusting Your Spring-Loaded Folders OS 9

OS 9: When you dragged a file into a folder (or from one folder to another) and paused for a moment over the destination folder, it would "spring open." This kept you from double-clicking through folder after folder, and it was a very popular feature. You could control the amount of time you had to pause over a folder before it "sprang" open by going to the Edit menu on the Finder's menu bar and selecting Preferences. Clicking on the General tab brought up the dialog shown above where you could set the delay time before a folder would spring open.

Adjusting Your Spring-Loaded Folders OS X

OS X: Now, you can control how long you have to pause over a folder before it springs open by going to the Finder menu and choosing Preferences. You can control the amount of delay before a folder springs open using the slider (as shown above). If you want the Spring-loaded feature turned off, click on the checkbox next to Spring-loaded folders and windows (it's on by default). By the way, when Mac OS X first shipped, the Spring-loaded folders feature wasn't in the first releases—it wasn't until Mac OS X 10.2 (Jaguar) that Spring-loaded folders made their appearance in Mac OS X. Just in case you care. You probably don't, but ya never know.

Chapter Four

 If you're a Mac user, chances are you are a "creative type." Someone my father might call a "hippy" but then, he is, after all, nearly 150 years old so I cut him some slack. For example, my dad (who is a genuinely wonderful man, and I firmly believe the father

Crank Up the Jams
MUSIC, PHOTOS, AND VIDEO

all fathers should be judged by) sadly still to this day uses the term "foxy" to describe an attractive-looking woman (he hasn't paid attention to any social vernacular since Laugh-in went off the air). In fact, I recently heard him call my wife "Foxy Mama" in a way that he hoped would sound complimentary. Well, my "Foxy Mama" is also a martial artist, and accordingly she beat him to a pulp. Hey, I can't say he didn't have it coming. Anyway, if you're a creative person (and I know you are), just silently pointing and clicking at text and icons isn't going to be enough for you. No, you need auditory and visual sensory stimulation. (If that sounds naughty, and it should, that makes you a bad person. Not me mind you. Just you. Bad, bad, bad!) Well, the next time you want to play a DVD (a naughty DVD no doubt), you'll need a little guidance on how things are done in Mac OS X (by the way, that's Mac OS "10" not "X," you sicko). That's what this chapter is all about—it's about getting music to play, video clips to run, DVDs to play, and the massive guilt you'll have from misusing these seemingly harmless tools.

Playing a Music CD OS 9

OS 9: Back in Mac OS 9, to play a music CD, you'd insert the CD in your CD-ROM drive, go under the Apple menu, and choose CDAudio Player. Then when it appeared, you'd click the Play button (as shown above). In the CDAudio Player preferences, under the Edit menu, you could check the box for Autoplay to have every audio CD begin playing as soon as you inserted them.

Playing a Music CD OS X

OS X: Now, by default, when you insert a music CD, Apple's iTunes application opens and begins playing the music CD. Insert the audio CD into your drive. When iTunes launches you will see a small CD icon in the Source Window at the left side of the iTunes window. Clicking on it will bring up a list of track names. Click on the first one you want to play and click the play arrow in the controller (top left). If you go to the iTunes Menu bar and select Controls, you can set such things as shuffle, repeat, etc. If you don't want to the CD to automatically play, just go under the Apple menu and choose System Preferences, then click on the CDs & DVDs icon to bring up those preferences. Then, where it says "When you insert a music CD" choose Ignore from the pop-up menu.

Pausing a CD Playing in the Background OS 9

OS 9: Back in Mac OS 9, if you were playing a music CD and wanted to pause it, you'd have to go the application menu, choose the Apple CD Player to make it the active application, then click the Pause button (as shown above).

Pausing a CD Playing in the Background OS X

OS X: Now, when a CD is playing in the background, you can pause it, switch to the next track, find out the name of the track, and a host of other handy controls without leaving your current application. Just click and hold (or Control-click) on the iTunes icon in the Dock, and a pop-up menu of controls will appear. To pause the audio CD, just choose Pause from the pop-up list.

Converting CDs to MP3 OS 9

OS 9: To convert your audio CDs to the MP3 format in Mac OS 9, you inserted your music CD into your drive and launched iTunes. You then selected the tracks you wanted to convert by clicking in the checkboxes next to their names. The final step was to click on the Import button in the top right corner of the iTunes window.

Converting CDs to MP3 OS X

OS X: You can convert your audio CDs to the MP3 format and save them on your hard drive to listen to anytime you want. Insert your audio CD and iTunes will launch. If you have an "always on" internet connection, the track names will appear in the playlist window (otherwise it will just say Track 1, Track 2, etc.). Make sure the checkboxes next to the tracks you want to convert are selected then click on the Import button in the top right corner of the iTunes window. iTunes will save your MP3s in the Music folder of your user account.

Burning Your Own Music CDs OS 9

OS 9: In Mac OS 9, if you wanted to burn a music CD, you'd open iTunes and arrange the tracks in the order you wanted them and make sure they were selected by clicking in the checkboxes by their titles. Once that was done, you inserted a blank CD and clicked the Burn CD button in the top right corner of the iTunes window.

Burning Your Own Music CD OS X

OS X: Now, you can sort and organize music and burn your own audio CDs directly from Apple's iTunes application (shown above). Start by inserting a music CD and choosing the songs you want to burn to CD (calling "ripping" in Apple slang), click on the New Playlist button at the bottom of the iTunes window, then drag the songs you have selected into this playlist. If you have songs you have previously ripped in your iTunes Library, drag them into this playlist as well. Arrange the songs in the order you want (called "mixing"), then click on the Burn CD button at the upper right corner of the iTunes window (shown above). You'll be prompted to insert a blank CD. Once you insert it, iTunes starts burnin'. (Called "Burn" in Apple slang. Oh, like you didn't see that comin'.)

Controlling External Speakers OS 9

OS 9: Back in OS 9, when you wanted to control external speakers connected to your Mac, you'd go under the Apple Menu, under Control Panels, and choose Sound to bring up the Sound Control Panel. Clicking on the Speakers tab opened the window shown above where you could make any adjustments you needed for your speakers (except make them sound really good).

Controlling External Speakers OS X

OS X: Now, you can control the balance, volume, and setup of external audio speakers connected to your Mac by going under the Apple menu, choosing System Preferences, and then clicking on the Sound icon to bring up the Sound Preferences. When the Sound Preferences pane appears, click on the Output tab and simply move the balance control to your liking.

Selecting an Audio Input Source OS 9

OS 9: Whenever you record audio on your Mac, you have to tell it where to "listen" for the signal. In Mac OS 9 you did this by going under the Apple Menu to Control Panels and selecting Sound. When the panel opened, you clicked on the Input tab and the window pictured above opened. From here you could select your input source (Built-in Mic, Internal CD, External Mic, etc.) and check the signal level before recording.

Selecting an Audio Input Source OS X

OS X: In Mac OS X you click on the Apple menu, select System Preferences, and choose Sound. When the Sound Preference pane opens, click on the Input tab and a list of available signal sources will be presented. Select the desired source by clicking on its name then adjust the signal input level with the Input volume adjustment slider.

Recording Audio from Your Mac OS 9

OS 9: Mac OS 9 included a wonderful little application (located in the Apple Extras folder) for recording CD-quality sound called SimpleSound. The length of your recordings was limited only by the amount of available hard drive space. To use SimpleSound, you first selected your signal input source (see page 94), chose a recording quality preset from the Sound menu, pressed Command-N to create a new file, and clicked the Record button on the SimpleSound controller (shown above). When you were done recording, you pressed the Stop button on the controller, clicked Save, and told your Mac where to save the file.

Recording Audio from Your Mac OS X

OS X: SimpleSound is gone in Mac OS X and has not been replaced with another application. If you want to do some recording, the easiest thing to do is to download a third-party
application (there are plenty of them available for free or for minimal Shareware fees).
There is one application on your Mac that you can use to record audio, though it's not
designed specifically for that purpose. iMovie has a voice-over feature which allows you to
record narration for your videos—well, you can also record narration even if you don't have
a video. Go to the Applications folder and launch iMovie. Click on the Audio button (if you
do not have an internal mic or have not attached an external source, it will be grayed out)
and then click the Record button. When you're done recording, click the button again and
save your file. Here's the crazy thing—you now have a movie file. If you want to use it as an
audio file you have to export it to another application (QuickTime for example) and convert
it to another file format. Want my advice? Download an audio application and save yourself
some time and trouble.

Accessing Photos from Your Digital Camera OS 9

OS 9: Back in Mac OS 9, when you needed to get your digital camera images onto your Mac, you would plug the cable that came with your camera into a USB port on your computer. In a few moments an icon would appear on your desktop (usually named Untitled). Clicking on the icon opened a window that usually contained a folder descriptively named DCIM. You clicked on this folder which opened yet another window containing a couple of folders, one of which had a name that bore some resemblance to the name of your camera. Clicking on this folder opened a window containing all your images labeled with names like DSCN0061, DSCN0062, DSCN0063, etc. You grabbed the ones you wanted and dragged them onto your desktop or into a folder on your hard drive.

Accessing Photos from Your Digital Camera OS X

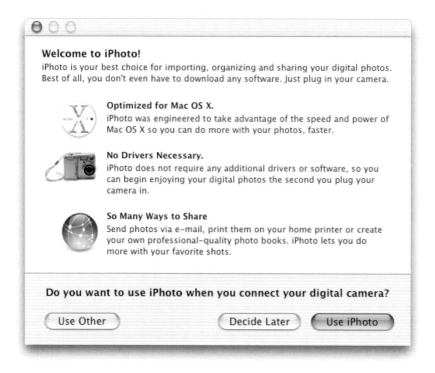

Welcome to iPhoto!

iPhoto is your best choice for importing, organizing and sharing your digital photos. Best of all, you don't even have to download any software. Just plug in your camera.

Optimized for Mac OS X.

iPhoto was engineered to take advantage of the speed and power of Mac OS X so you can do more with your photos, faster.

No Drivers Necessary.

iPhoto does not require any additional drivers or software, so you can begin enjoying your digital photos the second you plug your camera in.

So Many Ways to Share

Send photos via e-mail, print them on your home printer or create your own professional-quality photo books. iPhoto lets you do more with your favorite shots.

Do you want to use iPhoto when you connect your digital camera?

Use Other   Decide Later   Use iPhoto

OS X: Now, in Mac OS X, the first time you connect (via USB or Firewire) a digital camera or memory card reader to your Mac, the window shown above opens asking which application you would like to set as your default application for handling digital photos. The next time you hook up a camera or insert a media card, the application you selected will automatically open and download your photos to whatever folder you have designated. It just doesn't get much easier.

new stuff: *One of the best things about Mac OS X is the ability to use iPhoto. This amazing application is free and is packed with features that make it easy to download, catalog, view, edit, and share your digital photos.*

Taking Screen Captures OS 9

OS 9: In Mac OS 9 when you wanted to capture an image of what you were seeing on your screen, you pressed Shift-Command-3. If you wanted just a portion of the screen, the command was Shift-Command-4. This brought up a tiny crosshair which you could drag to select the portion of the screen image you wanted to capture. The capture images were saved to your desktop as .PICT files.

Taking Screen Captures OS X

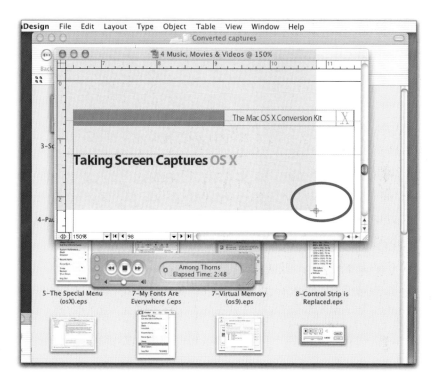

OS X: You can take a screen capture of the entire screen by pressing Shift-Command-3. If you want just a portion of the screen press Shift-Command-4. A crosshair will appear (see above) which you can drag over the portion of the screen you want to capture. As you drag, the portion you are selecting dims slightly (indicated by the arrows below). When you release your mouse a file will be saved on your desktop in .PDF format. Mac OS X includes a nifty little application named Grab, (it's inside the Utilities folder within the Applications folder). You can use Grab to take "regular" screen captures but it also has a timed feature which delays the capture for 10 seconds to give you time to open a window or menu that you want to capture. Grab saves the captures as .tif files, which you can open with Preview or another application of your choosing.

Viewing Graphics Files OS 9

OS 9: Back in Mac OS 9, when you clicked on a generic graphics file (one not tied to a particular application) it would open with one of several built-in applications, depending on
the file type. PictureViewer (located in the QuickTime folder) generally opened .jpeg files
while SimpleText opened .gif images. Once the images opened, you really had very little
control over them, but it was a handy way to see an image quickly.

Viewing Graphics Files OS X

OS X: In Mac OS X, Picture Viewer has been replaced by a much more powerful application—Preview. In addition to just opening files, Preview will combine multiple images
and allow you to preview them as thumbnails (see above). It also allows you to view your
selected images as a simple slide show. Finally, with Preview, you can export images to all
the main graphics formats. You can open a .jpg file, for instance, and export it as a .tif file.
Very handy when you need to convert from one format to another.

Playing QuickTime Movies OS 9

OS 9: Back in Mac OS 9, to watch a QuickTime movie, all you did was double-click on the movie's icon and a QuickTime player window opened on your desktop.

Playing QuickTime Movies OS X

OS X: Watching QuickTime movies is really pretty much the same in Mac OS X, but there are a couple of new things that are very convenient. If you set your window view to Column View (see page 27) you can preview movies without having to open them in QuickTime. If you have several movies and you're not sure which is the one you want to use, this is a real timesaver. Another new feature in Mac OS X is the ability to minimize a QuickTime movie to the Dock and still have it play. Okay, it's not one of those technology breakthroughs that is going to change life as we know it—but it is pretty cool.

Accessing Your DVD Player OS 9

OS 9: Back in OS 9, you launched your Apple DVD Player, you'd go under the Apple menu and choose Apple DVD Player. Simple enough.

Accessing Your DVD Player OS X

OS X: Now in OS X, you'll find it with your Applications Folder (as shown above). However, by default the DVD player will appear automatically anytime a DVD is inserted in your DVD drive. If for some reason you want this automatic DVD player launch turned off, you can do so by going under the Apple Menu, under System Preferences, and then clicking on the CDs & DVDs icon. There's a pop-up menu to the right of the words "When you insert a video DVD." From this list choose Ignore and then when you insert a DVD, your Mac will, well…do nothing—it will just ignore it and go on with its life.

Watching a DVD on Your Mac OS 9

OS 9: Back in Mac OS 9, when you inserted a DVD and wanted to watch it, you'd go under the Apple menu and choose Apple DVD player. This would bring up the round DVD player (shown above), and you could play the DVD by clicking on the Play button in the center of the controller.

Watching a DVD on Your Mac OS X

Clicking on the three little dots on the controller slides out a drawer with more options.

OS X: Now, by default, Apple's DVD player (shown above) appears automatically. (After all, it figures if you inserted a DVD into your Mac, you probably want to watch it, right?) To play the DVD, just press the Play button (highlighted above) on the cool-looking controller. If you don't want the DVD to automatically launch when you insert a DVD, just go under the Apple menu and choose System Preferences, then click on the CDs & DVDs icon to bring up those preferences. Then, where it says "When you insert a video DVD" choose Ignore from the pop-up menu (as shown above right).

Chapter Five

 Now, if someone walks up to you on the street and says, "Hey, what's a display?", you'd probably answer, "Something in a store window, or perhaps on a counter to showcase a product for sale." At least

Monitors

THEY'RE CALLED DISPLAYS IN MAC OS X

that's the kind of answer you'd give if you worked for an ad agency. Now, let's ask a regular person. I'll go ask Sarah Hughes, our company's staff writer and head of PR. Why Sarah? Because Sarah's desk is probably the closest to mine, and I can see from here that she's at her desk. Just a moment while I go and ask her, "What's a display?" I'll be right back. Okay, you're not going to believe this. Sarah said (and I swear this is true), "It's something set up to showcase products." However, truth be told, I think Sarah once worked for an ad agency, so her answer may have been skewed. So, if that's the definition of a display, what's the definition of a monitor? Sarah has now left her desk, so I'll have to go over to Paul's desk (also close by) to ask him the question, "What's a monitor?" I'll be right back. Okay, as expected, Paul said, "It's a computer monitor." It's pretty clear to everyone (meaning at least Paul and me) that the word "display" means "something in a store" and the word "monitor" means "computer monitor." But if a rose by any other name would smell as sweet, a monitor called a display is still as bright. I have a theory about why Apple calls monitors displays: it's all part of a plot to get you into the Apple Stores (found at pricier malls) by using the psychological camouflage of the word "display." Hey, it's not that far-fetched.

Setting Monitor Brightness OS 9

OS 9: Back in Mac OS 9, to set the brightness of your monitor you would go under the Apple menu, to Control Panels, and choose Monitors. This brought up the Control Panel shown above, and at the bottom left-hand corner was a slider for controlling the overall brightness of your monitor.

Setting Display Brightness OS X

OS X: Now you set the overall brightness for your display (monitor) by going under the Apple menu and choosing System Preferences. In the System Preferences window, click on the icon for Displays. When the Displays preference pane appears, use the Brightness slider in the lower left-hand corner to adjust overall brightness (as shown).

Choosing Your Monitor's Resolution OS 9

OS 9: Back in Mac OS 9, to change the resolution of your Mac's monitor, you'd go under the Apple menu, to the Control Panels folder, and choose Monitor. When the Monitor Control Panel opened, you'd choose your desired resolution from the list of available resolutions (your choices are limited by the size of your monitor, and the available video RAM installed on your Mac).

Choosing Your Display's Resolution OS X

OS X: Now to choose the resolution for your display you go under the Apple menu, launch System Preferences, and click on the Displays icon to bring up the pane shown above. Click on the Display tab, and choose your desired resolution from the list on the left side of the pane. You can choose any resolution that isn't "grayed" out.

new stuff: *If you have the Show displays in menu bar checkbox turned on, you'll also be able to choose your resolution setting from the menu bar at the top right corner of your screen. You can also set the color depth (Thousands or Millions of colors) and open the Displays preference pane.*

Thu 9:58 PM
Detect Displays
800 x 600
800 x 640
1024 x 768

Choosing Thousands or Millions of Colors OS 9

OS 9: To choose how many colors your monitor would display, back in Mac OS 9 you'd go under the Apple menu, to the Control Panels folder, and choose Monitor. When the Monitor Control Panel opened, you'd choose how many colors to display. *Note:* One reason to lower the number of colors displayed was to increase performance.

Choosing Thousands or Millions of Colors OS X

OS X: Now, you go under the Apple menu and choose System Preferences. Click on the Displays icon to bring up the Displays preferences panel. There's a pop-up list of color choices in the upper right-hand corner of the pane (as shown above). Just choose the one you want and close the pane.

Using Two Monitors OS 9

OS 9: If you have a video card capable of supporting two monitors, Mac OS 9 gave you the ability to either mirror the two displays (both would have the same image) or to arrange them to function like one big monitor. Mirroring was good for things like running a video projector because it allowed you to see the same image on your screen as the projector was displaying. Arranging the displays side-by-side (shown above) created a bigger desktop workspace.

Using Two Displays OS X

OS X: If your Mac is capable of supporting multiple displays (you may need to install a second graphics card), go under the Apple menu and choose System Preferences. Click on the Displays icon to open the Displays preferences pane. If you have more than one display connected, click the Detect Displays button (not visible if you have only one display) to open a dialog where you can choose how you want the displays to function. If you want both displays to have the same image, check the box to turn on Video Mirroring. With some Macs, it may be necessary to put the computer to sleep and wake it up before it will detect the second display. You shouldn't have to do a restart, however.

Putting Your Monitor to Sleep OS 9

OS 9: In Mac OS 9 when you wanted to set your monitor to go to sleep after a period of inactivity you went to the Apple menu, Control Panels, Energy Saver. This brought up a dialog with a single Energy Use slider. To configure the settings for your display, you clicked on the Show Details button in the lower right corner. This brought up the big dialog pictured above which allowed you to set separate sleep settings for your entire system, monitor, and hard drive.

Putting Your Display to Sleep OS X

If you are not using a PowerBook, the two drop-down menus at the top and the battery information at the bottom won't be visible when you open the Energy Saver preferences.

OS X: Now, to put your display to sleep to save battery and/or extend the life of your display, you go under the Apple menu and choose System Preferences. Then click on the Energy Saver icon to bring up the Energy Saver preferences pane. Click on the Sleep tab, then click the checkbox for Use separate time to put the display to sleep. Use the slider just below the checkbox (as shown above) to choose the delay before your display goes to sleep.

new stuff:	*If you're using a PowerBook, there's a checkbox at the bottom of this window that adds an item to your menu bar (up in the right-hand top corner of your display, near the menu bar clock) that lets you see how much battery life is left. If you click and hold on this menu item, a pull-down menu appears where you can choose to open the Energy Saver preferences pane. Mighty handy.*

Choosing Your Monitor Profile OS 9

OS 9: Back in Mac OS 9, you chose your monitor color profile by going under the Apple menu, into the Control Panels folder, and choosing Monitors, to bring up the dialog shown above. Clicking on the button labeled Color brought up a list of installed profiles to pick from.

Choosing Your Display Profile OS X

OS X: Now, you go under the Apple menu, choose System Preferences, and click on the Displays icon. In the Displays preference pane, click on the Color tab to bring up the pane shown above. Choose the profile appropriate for your display and the dialog shown above will appear. Choose a Profile from the list of built-in profiles (as shown).

Calibrating Your Monitor OS 9

OS 9: Back in Mac OS 9 to calibrate your monitor you'd go to the Apple menu, open Contol Panels and choose Monitors. When the dialog opened you clicked on the Color button to bring up a list of monitor profiles then clicked the Calibrate button at the bottom of the dialog. This brought up the Monitor Calibration Assistant (pictured above) which walked you through the steps to calibrate your monitor.

Calibrating Your Display OS X

OS X: Now, to calibrate your display you go under the Apple menu and choose System Preferences. In the System Preferenes window, click on the Displays icon to bring up the Displays preference pane. When it opens, click on the Colors tab. In the Colors tab, click on the Calibrate button, and the Display Calibrator Assistant (shown above) will appear and lead you through the step-by-step process of calibrating your display.

Chapter Six

Okay, why did I put printing and fonts together in the same chapter? Is it because these two have so much in common, or is it because these are two incredibly boring subjects? (Hint: it's fonts and printing.

Fonts and Printing
PERHAPS NOT THE MOST FUN CHAPTER

What do you think?) Hey, this isn't as bad as what I originally had planned for this chapter, which was facial exfoliation and printing. See, *now* printing sounds like fun. Luckily, in Mac OS X printing is about the easiest it's ever been. In fact, I doubt there's ever been a platform in the history of computers whose printing set-up has been easier and more intuitive than Mac OS X's. For example, when I wanted to connect my Mac to a network printer, I just called Brian (our in-house IT), he came to my office, and messed with some cables and dialogs while I was out to lunch. When I came back, son-of-a-gun the whole thing was up and running— and I could access all our printers. See, that's pretty easy, and that's what this chapter is all about—the easy way to print and install fonts in Mac OS X, like you used to do in Mac OS 9. For example, back in OS 9 there was no Brian. He didn't work for us, so I had to do everything myself. I was down on the ground, behind my G4, plugging in cables (and cussing), but it wasn't long after the launch of Mac OS X that we hired Brian, and since then, printing has become much easier. Coincidence? I think not.

Installing Fonts OS 9

OS 9: In Mac OS 9 when you wanted to install fonts, all you had to do was select the font(s) you wanted to install, drag them on top of the System folder, and drop them in. A dialog popped up letting you know that the fonts were going to be put in the Fonts folder. It was pretty much a no-brainer.

Installing Fonts OS X

Available to everyone with a user account on your Mac.

Available only to the person logged into this user account.

OS X: In Mac OS X it's still as easy as just dragging and dropping the fonts into a folder; the only tricky part is which folder, because there's more than one Fonts folder. If you're the only person that uses your Mac, you can drop them in the Fonts folder that appears inside the Library folder. You can also install fonts here if you share your Mac with other people, and you want these other people to all have access to these fonts. However, if you share your Mac with other users and want your own separate fonts (in other words, you're stingy and don't want to share), then instead you'd drag and drop your fonts into a different place. Go to your Users folder, then to your individual Home folder, then look in the Library folder (that's inside your Home folder) for a folder named Fonts. Drop 'em in there, and then these fonts will be available only to you when you log in.

new stuff:	*Didn't you hate it in Mac OS 9 when you had to quit an application before it could use the font you just installed? With Mac OS X any fonts you install are available to use immediately— even for applications that are already running. However, if the application you're using is running in Classic, you're going to have to do it the old fashioned way before the fonts will be available to you—quit both the application and Classic and restart them.*

Organizing Fonts OS 9

OS 9: In Mac OS 9 there really wasn't much you could do to organize your fonts other than sorting them by name, kind, etc.

Organizing Fonts OS X

OS X: One feature of Mac OS X that helps with font organization is the ability to keep fonts together in folders within the Fonts folder. That doesn't sound like such a big deal, but if you tried it in Mac OS 9, the System would not recognize them. It would look in the Fonts folder, see your neatly organized folders and say, "Hey—these aren't fonts, they're folders. What do you expect me to do with folders?" Mac OS X understands your need for organization. If it looks in the Font folder and sees another folder, it looks in it and opens any fonts it finds. Don't push it, though. It will only look one level deep.

new stuff:	*Mac OS X provides basic font management through the Font Panel. In Mac OS X-native applications (also known as Cocoa applications), such as Text Edit, you can access the Font Panel from the Format menu item (on the app's menu bar) or by pressing Command-T. It's limited (hey, it's free!) but does give you the ability to make font collections, preview typefaces and see all the characters available for a font.*

Selecting a Printer OS 9

OS 9: Designating a printer was something you seemed to have to do often in Mac OS 9. Fortunately it was easy. You just went to the Apple Menu and selected Chooser. When the Chooser dialog opened (pictured above) you clicked on the icon for the printer you wanted to use. It wasn't hard, but it was a pain because you had to do this every time you wanted to use a different printer.

Selecting a Printer OS X

OS X: In Mac OS X when you tell a document to print, the Print dialog opens. At the top is a pop-up menu showing the name of the currently selected printer. If that's the one you want to use, click the Print button. To select a different printer, click on the pop-up menu and choose the one you want from the list that opens. Don't see the one you want? Select Edit Printer List... and add the printer you want to use (see page 135). If you're a speed freak, the next time you're printing something, click on the Print Center icon in the Dock and choose Keep in Dock from the pop-up menu.

Adding a Printer OS 9

OS 9: In Mac OS 9 you can add as many printers as you liked by installing the drivers provided by the manufacturer. You could always tell which drivers were installed by going to the Apple Menu and selecting the Chooser. If a printer's icon was visible in the Chooser, its driver was installed.

Adding a Printer OS X

OS X: Adding printers in Mac OS X is pretty much the same except that it comes with a ton of drivers already installed. Before you go to the trouble of downloading and installing a driver for your printer, just connect it to your Mac and try printing a document. Chances are pretty good that it will just work. What a concept! From any application, press Command-P to bring up the box pictured here. Click on the Printer pop-up menu and select Edit Printer List…. When the list of current printers opens, click on the Add icon. If you click on the pop-up menu at the top, you will see a list of the ways a printer can be connected to your Mac. If you're using your basic ink jet, odds are it's hooked up to one of your USB ports. Select one of the connection options and choose your printer from the list that opens.

new stuff:	*If hard drive space is an issue for you and you want to get rid of the printer drivers you don't anticipate needing, go to the main Library and locate a folder named Printers. Open it up and locate the drivers you want to keep. Select all the others and drag them to the trash (or hit Command-Delete). I just did that on this iBook and got rid of 218.7 MB!*

Sharing a Printer OS 9

OS 9: In order to share a printer connected to your Mac with other people on your network you went to the Apple Menu to Control Panels and opened USB Printer Sharing. Once it was open, you clicked on the Start button in the lower section of the window. You also had to install a driver for your printer that allowed it to be accessed over a network.

Sharing a Printer OS X

OS X: In Mac OS X, setting your Mac to share its printer is done in the Sharing Preferences pane. From the Apple Menu, click on System Preferences and choose Sharing. When the pane pictured above opens, select Printer Sharing by clicking in its checkbox, then click the Start button. If AppleTalk is not active you will need to enable it before your printer can be shared, (see page 139).

Making AppleTalk Active OS 9

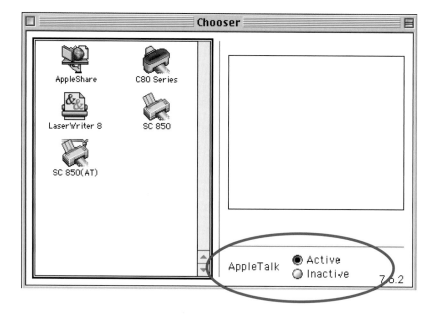

OS 9: To activate AppleTalk back in OS 9, you'd go under the Apple menu and select Chooser. In the lower right corner of the Chooser window were two buttons enabling you to make make AppleTalk active or inactive.

Making AppleTalk Active OS X

OS X: In Mac OS X the only thing you need AppleTalk for is to share a printer that is con-nected to another computer on your network (as opposed to being connected to the network directly). To enable AppleTalk, from the Apple Menu choose System Prefer-ences. When the System Preferences pane appears, click on the Network icon. Click on the AppleTalk tab (as shown above), then click the checkbox labeled Make AppleTalk Active, near the top of the pane.

Viewing the Print Queue OS 9

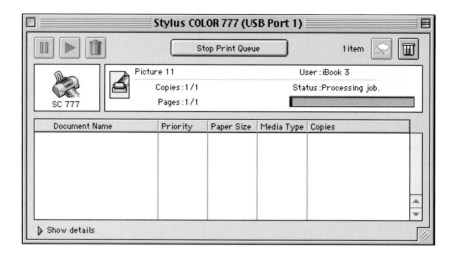

OS 9: In Mac OS 9 every time you told a document to print, the OS secretly launched an application called Print Monitor. The document spooled to the Print Monitor, which then sent it to whatever printer was selected. If you wanted to see what was in the print queue or changed your mind and wanted to stop the presses, you clicked on the active applications menu (top right corner of your screen) and chose Print Monitor. If you were really fast and got it opened before your document was sent to the printer you had the opportunity to cancel, rearrange, or hold until a specific time.

Viewing the Print Queue OS X

OS X: In Mac OS X when you tell a document to print, it launches an application called Print Center—no sneaking around here, you can see Print Center right on your Dock. That's the only way you'll know it's running because it won't open a window and take over your screen. If you want to see the print queue, however, simply click on Print Center's Dock icon and it will open a window showing you a list of all current printing activity.

new stuff:	*When you open Print Center, it will show you the status of any active printers. Double-clicking on the name of a printer will bring up a detail window (right) showing information about all jobs queued to it.*	

Chapter Seven

 I know why you came to this chapter. You're looking for fun, aren't you? And you know down deep in your soul that when it comes to sheer unadulterated fun, there's nothing like a chapter on networking.

Networking and the Internet

HOW COULD THIS BE ANYTHING BUT A PARTY?

It's kind of like a "Macs Gone Wild on Spring Break" video (only without the video, or spring break, or anything even remotely wild). Admittedly, a chapter on networking would be almost as boring as a chapter on printing and fonts, (don't worry, I would never write a boring chapter like Printing and Fonts, so whatever you do, don't look at Chapter 6 "Fonts and Printing"). Anyway, since I knew I was going to have to cover networking, I thought I'd better find a more exciting topic to go with it to help offset the innate boringness of networking. *(Note to Editor: If "boringness" isn't actually a word, use "boralating" instead.)* So, in short, I added the flashy, exciting, Vegas-a-go-go world of the Internet to this boring networking chapter. This will create what will go down in history as either a brilliant marriage of two polar opposite topics to create a "swingin' über-chapter," or it could turn out to be a topic-ganging calamity which shall bear the eternal mark of shame. *(Whispered: Little do they know, that the Internet part of this chapter may actually eclipse the networking part in terms of "boring info per square inch" because the Internet part is about TCP/IP settings, IP Addresses, etc., and there's little or no mention of Vegas. Of course, I would never admit to that, because it might hurt book sales.)*

Sharing Your Mac with Other Users OS 9

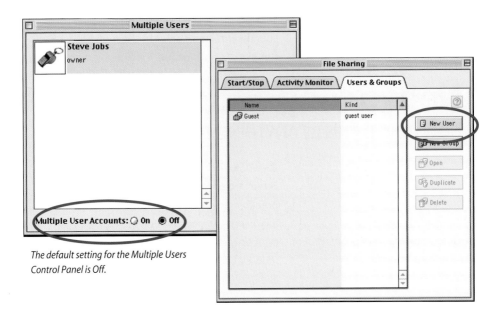

The default setting for the Multiple Users Control Panel is Off.

OS 9: In Mac OS 9 you had the ability to set up user accounts on your Mac by going to the Control Panels and opening Multiple Users. After clicking the On button, you opened the File Sharing Control Panel, clicked on the Users and Groups tab, and added the new users.

Sharing Your Mac with Other Users OS X

OS X: In Mac OS X to add a user, go to the Apple Menu to System Preferences and click on Accounts. When the pane opens, click the New User button. A new pane will open (see above) which allows you to enter the information for the new user. If you want this user to be allowed to administer the computer, check the box at the bottom of the pane.

Setting User Privileges OS 9

OS 9: In Mac OS 9 if you wanted someone to be able to use your Mac, but didn't want to give them carte blanche, you could assign privileges. This could be as general as "Cannot use CD drive" or as specific as which applications they were allowed to use. To set the privileges you went to the Apple Menu, selected Control Panels and clicked on Users and Groups. When the dialog opened and you selected a user, the window shown above opened and you could set the options however you desired.

Setting User Privileges OS X

OS X: In Mac OS X you can assign privileges for any user who is not an administrator. From the Apple Menu, select System Preferences and choose Accounts. When the list of users appears, select one and click the Capabilities button. From the window that opens you will be able to set that user's privileges. You might think that if you're not in an office environment you wouldn't have much use for this feature. Watch your four-year-old clicking and dragging stuff all over the desktop someday and you'll realize it has broader application than you thought.

Controlling Access OS 9

OS 9: In Mac OS 9 if you wanted to control access to certain areas of your computer (as opposed to setting privileges for individual users), you could set up groups and set the level of access for the entire group. This was a lot easier than having to do it for every user. You could, for instance, have groups for Marketing, Accounting, Sales, etc. Any user who was in the Sales group would have whatever privileges were assigned to that group. Users could be in more than one group, but did not have to be in any group. It got pretty complicated. It also didn't protect any of your personal files and it was pretty easy for other users in your group to modify or delete them.

Controlling Access OS X

OS X: Access to files in Mac OS X is controlled in large part by where the files are stored. Files saved in certain areas (the main Library and System folder, for example) are accessible only to persons having administrator privileges. There are areas which can be accessed by anyone on a network and areas open to anyone who has an account on the particular Mac. Then there are user accounts—accessible only to the owner (and anyone with whom they have shared their login information). Fully explaining it is way beyond the scope of this book, but it's something you'll want to get at least a basic understanding of. It can be a bit confusing at first (especially when you try to delete a file and are told you don't have sufficient permission) but once you understand the big picture you'll appreciate how easy it is to keep your files safe and private.

Sharing Your Files OS 9

OS 9: In Mac OS 9, to share files on your Mac with other users on your network, you went to the Apple menu, selected Control Panels and chose File Sharing. After entering the Network Identity information, you clicked the Start button.

Sharing Your Files OS X

OS X: In Mac OS X, from the Apple menu, select System Preferences and choose Sharing. When the Sharing Preference pane (shown above) opens, click in the box next to Personal File Sharing.

Connecting to a Network: Configuring OS 9

OS 9: There were two steps in the process of configuring your Mac for connecting to a net-work in Mac OS 9. The first was to open the TCP/IP Control Panel and enter your IP address and DNS server information. The second step was to open the AppleTalk Control Panel and select the type of network you were connecting to: Ethernet, LocalTalk, or AirPort (if you were connecting to an AirPort network, you had to open the AirPort Control Panel and configure it as well). There was an additional third step which was sometimes part of the network configuration process in Mac OS 9—cussing more times than you usually do dur-ing 18 holes of golf when you couldn't connect to the network after setting everything up.

Connecting to a Network: Configuring OS X

OS X: In Mac OS X you only need to open one preference to configure your network (two if you are going wireless). From the Apple menu, select System Preferences, click on Network and the preference pane shown above opens. If you had already configured your network settings in Mac OS 9, you'll see that Mac OS X has taken the liberty of entering the information already. Erase it! What an insult. You're no wimpy, lightweight computer user. You're no fool, either, so if the information's correct, leave it alone. If the information is not already entered, contact your network administrator or Internet Service Provider and ask them for the information, then enter it manually. If you're going to be connecting to Macs that are not using Mac OS X, you will need to enable AppleTalk by clicking on its tab and selecting the appropriate checkbox in the window that opens.

Connecting to a Network OS 9

OS 9: To connect to a local network in Mac OS 9, you went to the Apple menu and selected Chooser. When the Chooser opened (assuming you had configured your network settings) you saw an icon for AppleShare. Clicking on this icon brought up a list of any computers currently available. You selected the one you wanted, entered any user information and password, and you would be connected.

Connecting to a Network OS X

OS X: In Mac OS X, since there is no Chooser, you go to the Finder's Menu bar and click on Go. When the pull-down menu opens, scroll to the bottom and select Connect to Server. This opens the window shown above where you simply click on the desired server and click Connect. If you have an account on the server, enter your login information. If not, you can log in as a guest.

new stuff:	One great new feature of Mac OS X is the Drop box. If you are on a network and need to send another user a file you are working on, but don't have an account on their computer, you can put the file in their Drop box. Here's how: Connect to their computer as a guest which will put an icon on your desktop for their user account. Click on the icon and you will see a folder labeled Drop Box. Just drag any files you want to send to them to their Drop box. You won't be able to see them, but they will be able to access them by going to the Public folder inside their user account.

AirPort: Going Wireless OS 9

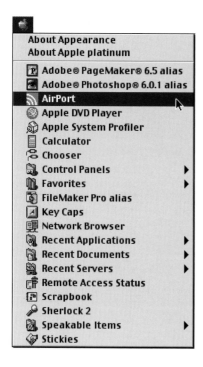

OS 9: Back in OS 9, you'd turn on AirPort wireless access by going under the Apple menu, and right at the top was AirPort. You'd click on it, and it would open the AirPort Control Panel.

AirPort: Going Wireless OS X

OS X: Now, you can Access AirPort from the System Preferences, but there's a better way if you use AirPort a lot. You have to set it up (just once) by going under the Apple menu and choosing System Preferences. When the System Preferences panel appears, click on the Network icon; then where it says "Show," choose AirPort from the pop-up menu. (*Note:* If you don't have an AirPort card installed, AirPort won't be one of the choices.) Then click on the AirPort tab, and at the bottom of the AirPort panel is a checkbox to Show Airport Status in Menu Bar. Turn this checkbox on, and you'll be able to turn AirPort on/off, access various networks, and even open the Preferences by clicking and holding on the icon.

Setting Internet Preferences OS 9

OS 9: To set up your Mac to be able to connect to the Internet in Mac OS 9 you opened the Control Panels from the Apple Menu and chose the Internet Control Panel. The somewhat confusing dialog shown above opened and allowed you to enter information for your e-mail account and other online services.

Getting Ready to Go Online OS X

OS X: If you haven't already configured your Network Preferences, you will need to do that first, (see page 153). Next, from the Apple menu, select System Preferences, choose Internet and the pane shown above will open. Click on the E-mail tab and enter the information about your account. Next, plug your Ethernet cable into the wall jack and you're ready to go online.

new stuff:	*You probably noticed the three-inch high .mac logo in the Internet Preferences pane. This is the new online service rolled out by Apple that has a plethora of features and services. There are some handy features, so it's worth checking out. Just click the Sign up button in the lower right corner to connect to the .mac site and get more information.*

Setting Up Your Modem OS 9

Mac OS 9: Before you could connect to a network with your modem in Mac OS 9, you had to set your modem preferences. To do that you went under the Apple menu to Control Panels and selected Modem. The window shown above opened and you selected your modem from the drop-down list, set the sound and dialing options, and decided to require or ignore a dial tone.

Setting up Your Modem OS X

Mac OS X: The modem preferences in Mac OS X are accessed from the Network Preferences pane. From the Apple menu, select System Preferences and choose Network. When the pane opens, click on the drop-down menu labeled Show and select Modem port. Click on the Modem tab and choose your modem from the drop-down menu at the top.

Searching on the Internet OS 9

OS 9: In OS 9, you could use Sherlock 2 (the built-in Find function) to seach the Internet as long as you had an active Internet connection. You'd just press Command-F to bring up Sherlock 2, then you'd click one of the icons across the top (except the first one, your hard drive), and you could do a basic search (using some of the popular Web search engines), or you could search for people, shop for items, news, search Apple's Web site, Dictionary, movie times, and even create your own custom search channels.

Searching on the Internet OS X

OS X: Now, Sherlock is exclusively for searching the Web, and it does not perform searches of your hard drive or local disks. Again, you click on the icon for the type of search you want to perform, type in your search term, then hit the Search button. Why would you use this instead of one of the regular online search engines? You wouldn't for most things, but if you're looking for movie times, for instance, Sherlock rocks. Once it knows your ZIP code, it brings up every movie at every theater in your area. Click on the one you're thinking about and a short description and a QuickTime trailer pop up. How cool is that?

Chapter Eight

 Now, where would you put stuff that really didn't fit into the other categories? That's right, into a Miscellaneous chapter, but I'm not a big fan of the word "miscellaneous." I even prefer the shorter "misc.," especially

Other Stuff
THE LAND OF LITTLE LOST COMMANDS

since there's a reasonable chance that I'll misspell miscellaneous most of the time; so I switched the chapter title to "Other Stuff." I know what you're thinking—"…but Scott, you've got a spell checker, right?" While it's true that I have a spell checker, I seldom use it. Why? Because I have editors. Not just one editor mind you, multiple editors, and it's their job to (a) check my spelling manually, and (b) make me sound significantly smarter than I am. (For example, originally I didn't use the words "significantly smarter," I used the words "more smartest.") However, while you're reading this, you're probably thinking "Ya know, Scott really doesn't sound all that smart." That's simply because I don't pay my editors enough. Why don't I pay them more (you might ask)? It's because they're stealing from me. Constantly. For example, I'll go into my office on a particular day, and my pen will be missing. Of course, I go straight to my editors and announce, 'Hey, my pen's missing," and they all get this look on their face like "We didn't take it." But that goes against the ingrained nature of all editors, which is to lie when asked a direct question. Here's proof: I asked them, "Hey, how'd you like the intro copy for the "Misc. Stuff" chapter?" and they said "Great! Nice job. You've done it again." Clearly, they can't be trusted.

Ejecting a Disk OS 9

OS 9: Back in Mac OS 9, to eject a disk (an external hard drive, CD, Zip disk, etc.) you'd click on the icon of the disk you want to eject and either drag it to the Trash, or you could press Command-Y (the shortcut for Put Away). You could also choose Eject from the Special menu, but that feels so 1980s.

Ejecting a Disk OS X

OS X: The easiest way to eject a disk is to press the Eject button on your keyboard. If your keyboard doesn't have an Eject key, try holding down the F12 key. Need another option? Click on the disk's icon and drag it to the Trash. The Trash icon will immediately change to an Eject symbol (which mentally feels better than dragging a perfectly good disk into the trash) and the disk is ejected as soon as you release your mouse. You can also click on the disk's icon and go to the menu bar, select File and click on Eject. The keyboard shortcut for this is Command-E for Eject. (Much better than Command-Y, as in, "Y in the world was Command-Y the shortcut for ejecting a disk?") One more option for ejecting a disk—Control-click on the disk icon and select Eject from the contextual menu.

new stuff: *As soon as you start to drag a disk icon, the trash can turns to the Eject symbol because it assumes that's what you want to do. If you're just moving the icon don't worry—it won't eject the disk unless you drop it onto the Eject symbol.*

Removing an Item from the Apple Menu OS 9

OS 9: To remove an item from the Apple menu in Mac OS 9, you had to go to the System Folder, into the Apple Menu Items folder, and drag the item outside the folder (as shown above).

Removing an Item from the Dock OS X

OS X: In Mac OS X, to remove an item from the Dock, just click on the Dock icon and drag it right out of the Dock. An animated puff of smoke will appear to let you know it's removed. If you drag an item out and it snaps right back, it is either an open application or a document window which you have minimized. If it's an application, click and hold on the Dock icon and select Quit from the contextual menu. Once the application quits you will be able to drag it out of the Dock. If it's a window that's been minimized, click on it once to make it full-size, then click the red button in its top left corner to close it.

How Much Memory (RAM) Do You Have OS 9

OS 9: Back in Mac OS 9, to find out how much RAM you had, you went to the Apple Menu and selected About This Computer. When the screen pictured above opened, the amount of RAM you had installed was displayed as Built-in Memory.

How Much Memory (RAM) Do You Have OS X

The Apple System Profiler gives you more detail about your Mac's memory.

OS X: Now, in Mac OS X, you go under the Apple menu and choose About This Computer. A dialog will appear displaying the amount of installed RAM (as shown above). As you can see, the Mac shown here has 512 MB of RAM. In other words, it probably needs more RAM. How much more? A bunch. Honestly, just saying "a bunch" is kind of arbitrary. It's actually "a whole bunch." If you need more information than this, and you want to really dig under the hood and find out all the inner technical specs of your Mac (in other words, you spend a lot of time alone in your room), click on the More Info button and an application named Apple System Profiler will open and you'll be able to find out things like your Boot ROM info (mine is 4.3.7f3, just in case you were wondering). You will also be able to get useful information about your Mac.

Determining a File's Size OS 9

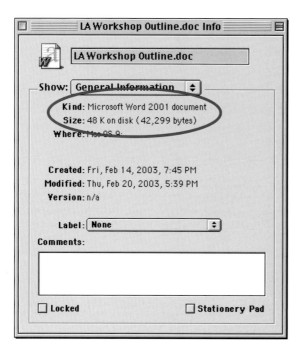

OS 9: Back in Mac OS 9, to quickly find out the size of any file, you could click on the file then press Command-I to bring up the file's Info window, where the file size would appear, as shown above. You could also see the file's size, in the Size column if the window (folder) it lived in was set to List view (rather than Icon view).

Determining a File's Size OS X

OS X: The same keyboard shortcut, Command-I (for Get Info), still applies in Mac OS X. Pressing it brings up the Get Info window (shown above) and the file size appears next to the word Size. If you want to see the file size without bringing up the Get Info box, you can set the window view to either List view or Column view and the size information will be displayed.

Adding Comments to a File OS 9

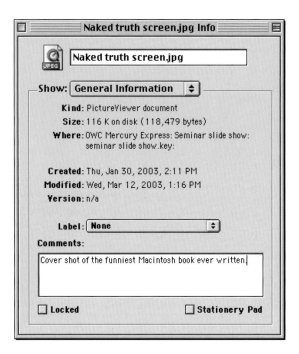

OS 9: Back in Mac OS 9, you could add your own personal comments to most any file by pressing Command-I and typing them into the Comments field at the bottom of the dialog. (By comments, I mean literally anything you want to say about the file, like "This file annoys me," "I was having a bad day when I created this file," "Don't forget to delete this file after Valentine's Day," etc.) You could only view these comments in the same way—clicking on the file and pressing Command-I (Get Info).

Adding Comments to a File OS X

OS X: Now, not only can you add comments, you can actually see these comments when viewing files in a Finder window set to List view. First, add your own comments by pressing Command-I to bring up the Info window; click on the disclosure triangle before the word "Comments"; and type your comments in the white box (as shown above left). To view these comments, open the folder that contains your file, click the View by List button, and press Command-J to bring up the View preferences for this window. Under Show, turn on the checkbox for Comments, and they'll now be visible in your window (above right).

Keeping a File from Being Deleted OS 9

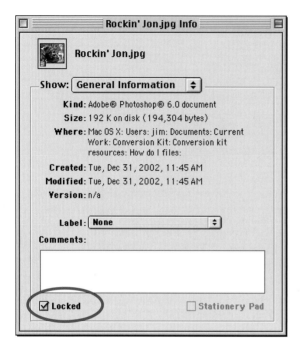

OS 9: Back in Mac OS 9, if you had a file you wanted to make sure didn't get accidentally deleted (trashed) from your hard drive, you could lock it by clicking on the file, then pressing Command-I to bring up the Get Info window. If you checked the box next to Locked, the file could be put in the Trash, but it wouldn't be deleted when you emptied the Trash.

Keeping a File from Being Deleted OS X

OS X: You still lock a file pretty much the same way but the protection is better in Mac OS X. Press Command-I to bring up the Info window, and then click the Locked checkbox (as shown above left). In OS 9, you could drag a locked file to the Trash but the Trash wouldn't empty (you'd get a warning that something was locked, but it wouldn't tell you which file). But in OS X, you can't even drag a locked file into the Trash in the first place. If you try, you'll get the "Oh no you don't" warning dialog.

new stuff:	Another new locking feature in OS X is that you now get a visible cue to tell you a file is locked. When you lock a file, it adds a tiny padlock to the left of its icon (as shown at right) so you no longer have to press Command-I just to see if a file's locked—you can just look at the icon. Nice.	

Getting Stuff out of the Trash OS 9

OS 9: Back in Mac OS 9, if you tossed something into the Trash and then decided you didn't want it in there after all, you could just double-click on the Trash icon on your Desktop. This would open the Trash window, and you could drag your file right out.

Getting Stuff out of the Trash OS X

OS X: Now, you can access the Trash window by going to the Dock and clicking once on the Trash icon. Drag the file you want to keep right out of the Trash window, just like in Mac OS 9. However, there's a great new feature that should keep you from digging in the Trash too often. If you drag a file to the Trash then immediately decide you want to keep it, you have an undo. That's right, just press Command-Z to undo the trashing of that file, and it will jump right back where it came from. Now, you only get one undo, so don't trash the file, then go off and do 15 other things, and hope to undo that file back out of the trash. At that point, you'd have to do it the old-fashioned way—double click on the Trash icon and go dumpster diving.

Changing a File's Icon OS 9

OS 9: In Mac OS 9, to copy an icon from one file to another, you'd start by clicking on the file whose icon you want to copy , then press Command-I to bring up the Get Info window. Then you'd click on the tiny icon that appears at the top left, press Command-C to copy it, then you'd close the Get Info window. Next, you would click on the file you wanted to have that icon, press Command-I to open its Info window, click on the icon at the top left of the window, and press Command-V to paste the icon you copied. Done. New icon.

Changing a File's Icon OS X

OS X: In Mac OS X the process is the same, your basic copy and paste. Click on the file whose icon you want to steal and press Command-I. Go to the top left corner of the Get Info box, click on the icon and press Command-C to copy it. Now find the file whose icon you want to change, press Command-I, click on the icon in the top left corner and press Command-V. (It's the shortcut for paste, which really makes very little sense, but life is like that sometimes.)

new stuff:	Here's a sweet trick—click once on the file whose icon you want to change. Now press Option-Command-I which brings up its Get Info window, select its icon and press Command-C to copy it. Now click on any other file and instead of opening a new Get Info box, the new file's info opens in the same window with its icon already highlighted. Click on as many files as you like , When their info appears, press Command-V and they have a whole new look.

Switching Applications OS 9

OS 9: Back in Mac OS 9, if you had more than one application open, you could switch from one to another by going to the Application Switcher at the top right-hand corner of your Menu bar, where the current application's name or icon was shown. You'd click on that name and a pop-down menu would appear (the infamous application switcher) and you'd switch to another open application by clicking on it in that list.

Switching Applications OS X

Command-Tab steps forward through open applications. Shift-Command-Tab reverses direction.

OS X: Now in Mac OS X, you switch to another open application by simply clicking on its icon in the Dock. If you're too lazy to move your cursor all the way to the bottom of your screen, you can step through your open applications (including the Finder) by pressing Command-Tab while in your current application (Shift-Command Tab reverses direction). Each time you press, you'll see the next Dock icon highlight and magnify. When the icon for the application you want to use is highlighted, release the Command and Tab keys and the new application will become active.

Accessing an Application's Preferences OS 9

OS 9: Back in Mac OS 9, you could access most applications' customizable preferences from the application's Edit menu. Now you might think, "Isn't it odd that software developers all over the world had the exact same idea about where preferences should go?" That would be odd—freaky even. But before you start calling talk radio shows to share your theory of a "One World Developer Alliance Conspiracy," let me present another possible explanation— Apple asked developers to put the preference settings there so it would be consistent among programs. But you can still call your radio program, because while the developers made it appear as if the preferences were in the Edit menu, they really weren't. The actual preference files were really in a folder buried in the System folder. The name of this secret folder? Preferences. Hang up the phone, not much of a conspiracy here. But what if they only want to make us think the preferences are in the Preferences folder? Hmmmmmm. Hand me the phone, Earl.

Accessing an Application's Preferences OS X

OS X: Now, Apple has asked software developers to place Preferences access under the Application menu (which is actually the name of the application itself, to the immediate right of the Apple Menu at the top left corner of the screen). In the example shown above, the open application is Adobe Photoshop. When you select Preferences, you are actually opening a file that is in the Application Support folder which is, in turn, in the System Library. Confused? That's exactly what they want.

Putting Your Mac to Sleep OS 9

OS 9: In Mac OS 9 you had two easy ways to put your computer to sleep. The first was to go to the Menu bar, select Special and choose Sleep from the drop-down menu. The second way was to click on the Control Strip, find the Energy Saver icon (the little crescent moon on a blue star field) and choose Sleep Now .

Putting Your Mac to Sleep OS X

OS X: It's still easy in Mac OS X. Now you click on the Apple menu and choose Sleep (as shown above).

new stuff: You can also press your Computer's Power On button to bring up a dialog box asking if you want to Restart, Shut Down, or Sleep. On some Macs, you can also press Control-Eject and the same choices will appear.

Keeping Your Mac from Going to Sleep OS 9

OS 9: Back in Mac OS 9, if you wanted to prevent your Mac from going to sleep on you (which was mostly a concern of PowerBook and iBook users), you poured three double-shot espressos on the keyboard. No wait, that's what happened when you were trying to stay awake to get your taxes done. To keep your Mac awake, you went to the Apple menu, selected Control Panels, and chose Energy Saver. When the Energy Saver Control Panel appeared, you clicked on the Show Details button in the lower right corner. When the dialog box opened all you had to do was move the appropriate sliders to Never.

Keeping Your Mac from Going to Sleep OS X

OS X: Now, you set your Mac's nap time in the Energy Saver Preference pane. Go under the Apple Menu and choose System Preferences, then click the Energy Saver icon. When the Energy Saver Preference pane appears, click on the Sleep tab and move the top slider to the far right, to Never. That's it—no more sleepy bear syndrome.

new stuff: *If you're using a PowerBook or iBook, Mac OS X has two Energy Saver pre-sets already configured—one for when your Power Adapter is plugged in (so you can pretty much turn sleep off for maximum performance) and another which puts battery conservation over performance and puts your Mac to sleep when it's not being used.*

Restarting Your Mac OS 9

OS 9: Back in Mac OS 9, you had to do a lot of restarting. Typically after you installed a new application, font, extension or control panel your Mac wouldn't "see" it until you restarted. The easiest way to do that was to go to the menu bar, click on Special, and choose Restart.

Restarting Your Mac OS X

OS X: With Mac OS X, most items you install are recognized and able to be used by your Mac without a restart. There are times when that's not the case, but most installers will warn you in advance so you can decide whether to go ahead with the install or wait. If you do need to restart, you now go under the Apple menu (as shown above) and select restart. On newer machines, pressing the Power On button will bring up a dialog where you can choose to Sleep, Shut Down, or Restart.

Shutting Down Your Mac OS 9

OS 9: Back in Mac OS 9, to shut down (when you were totally done working on your Mac for the day) you'd go under the Special Menu and choose Shut Down.

Shutting Down Your Mac OS X

When you choose Shut Down, by default it brings up a dialog asking "Are you sure you want to shut down your computer now?" You can stop this somewhat annoying dialog from appearing at all, by holding down the Option key before you choose Shut Down from the Apple Menu.

OS X: Now, you shut down by going under the Apple Menu and choosing Shut Down. On some Macs, you can shut down by pressing the Power button. This brings up a dialog where you can choose to Sleep, Restart, or Shut Down. On newer Macs, pressing the power button puts your Mac to sleep instantly. If you want to get the choices, press Control-Eject.

new stuff:	*One of the things about OS X that take some getting used to for some people is the fact that you really don't need to shut down your Mac unless you can't stand the thought of the pennies of electricity it is consuming on a monthly basis. When you're done for the day, let it run. Geeks routinely check Apple System Profiler to see how long their Mac has been running since the last restart. Since it is such a stable operating system, it's possible to go several weeks before you have to restart. Uptime, baby. It's all about uptime.*

Changing the Startup Disk OS 9

OS 9: Back "in the day" if you wanted to start up from a different drive than your current startup disk or if you wanted to start up from a different version of the operating system, you would go under the Apple menu, under Control Panels, and choose Startup Disk. The Startup Disk Control Panel would open (shown above) and you could choose to start up from any disk that had a Mac OS properly installed on it. This would often actually work.

Changing the Startup Disk OS X

OS X: Now, you choose your startup System (or disk) by going under the Apple menu and launching System Preferences. Then click on the Startup Disk icon. The Startup Disk Preference pane will appear, showing all available and valid System folders. Choose one and click the Restart button. Earlier Macs could boot from either OS 9 or OS X. Recent Macs will boot only in Mac OS X.

Chapter Nine

I've got to figure that, if you're reading this chapter, it's not because everything is working perfectly. You're probably here because there's a problem. Perhaps it's a dead-end job, an unfulfilling marriage, or

Troubleshooting
IT'S NOT A GOOD SIGN IF YOU'RE READING THIS

maybe it's a drinking problem. That's what it was for me. Drinking. Heavy drinking, brought on shortly after installing Mac OS X when I went looking for the familiar ambulance icon of Disk First Aid. I went straight to the Utilities folder (the warm fuzzy location it had been nearly all of my adult life), but it just wasn't there. I searched everywhere on my drive, but to no avail. I freaked. At that time, there was no book like this to tell me what happened to the little ambulance icon, so I turned to the bottle. It wasn't pretty. I remember feeling so detached, so disconnected from my previous OS experience that I let drinking get the best of me. The next morning I woke up to find myself lying half naked on the floor of a Mexican jail, with a WIndows XP installer disc in one hand and a map to Liza's house in the other. Needless to say, this was a serious wake-up call. Anyway, this chapter is probably not what it seems, because it's not about how to troubleshoot Mac OS X—every Mac book covers that—instead in keeping with the format of this book (how to do the same things you did in OS 9, but now in OS X), it's about where Apple secretly moved all the troubleshooting stuff you're already used to using—in a lightly veiled effort to get you to fall off the wagon.

Force Quitting an Application OS 9

Force "PictureViewer" to quit?
Clicking Force Quit causes you to lose any
unsaved changes. To avoid further problems,
restart your computer after you click Force
Quit.

(Force Quit) **Cancel**

OS 9: Back in OS 9, if an application froze up, you could Force Quit it—which if you were lucky would give you enough time to go to any other applications and save their open documents before you restarted (which you just about absolutely had to do, because after an application crash, you could be pretty sure that a system crash was on its way). To Force Quit an application, you'd press Command-Option-Esc. This would actually work about 50–60% of the time.

Force Quitting an Application OS X

OS X: Now, if an application freezes—no sweat, you can Force Quit it and then relaunch it and get right back to work—it doesn't take down the computer (like a Force Quit in OS 9 normally did). To Force Quit an open application, go under the Apple menu and choose Force Quit (or press the keyboard shortcut Command-Option-Esc.) This brings up the Force Quit dialog (shown above) and you can just click on the application you want to force quit, then click the Force Quit button (highlighted above).

new stuff:	You can also Force Quit an application by holding the Control and Option keys, then clicking on the applica- tion's icon in the dock. A pop-up menu will appear (as shown here) and you can choose Force Quit from here.	

Using Disk First Aid OS 9

OS 9: Back in OS 9, when your Mac started acting funky, you'd run Disk First Aid. This handy little utility could repair a host of little problems, that could turn into big problems. It was found in your Mac OS 9 Utilities folder, and its icon was a boxy-looking ambulance.

Using Disk First Aid OS X

OS X: Now, Disk First Aid is part of a utility called Disk Utility, which you will find in the Utilities folder inside your Applications folder. When you launch Disk Utility, click on the First Aid tab, then in the column on the left side of the dialog click on the drive you want to repair, then click the Repair Disk button. You can use First Aid to repair external drives, partitioned drives, etc., but not your startup drive (at least, not without going this next step). If you want to verify or repair your startup disk, you'll have to boot from your Mac OS X install CD. With the install CD in your drive, choose Restart from the Apple Menu, then hold down the C key to force your Mac to boot from the CD rather than the hard drive. Once the startup process begins, you can release the C key. When the installer window appears, go to the menu bar at the top of the screen, click on Installer and select Open Disk Utility to open the Disk Utility. (Did I really need to explain that part?) Now you'll be able to choose your startup drive for verification or repair.

Force Quitting the Finder OS 9

Force "Finder" to quit?
Clicking Force Quit causes you to lose any
unsaved changes. To avoid further problems,
restart your computer after you click Force
Quit.

OS 9: Back in Mac OS 9, if you wanted to Force Quit the Finder (rather than an application) you could, by going to the Finder and pressing Option-Command-Esc. A warning dialog "Are you sure you want to quit the Finder?" would appear, and you had a 50/50 chance of it force quitting and not bringing down your Mac (which is probably a higher percentage than you'd get an application to force quit and not crash your Mac).

Force Quitting the Finder OS X

OS X: Now, in Mac OS X if your Finder should get stuck, probably the fastest way to get it unstuck is to press Option-Command-Esc to bring up the Force Quit dialog (shown above). Click on Finder, then press the Relaunch button. Relaunch is probably a better term than Force Quit because it doesn't really quit the Finder; instead it relaunches the Finder (basically starts it up again). You may have to relaunch it several times before it will work. Don't ask why—it's just the way it is.

Booting from Your System CD OS 9

OS 9: When all else failed in Mac OS 9, you could always boot up your Mac from the System 9 Install CD. You inserted the CD into the drive, went to the Special menu and selected Restart then held down the C key to force the computer to boot from the CD instead of the hard drive. When the startup process was done, you could access all your drives and files. The only visible difference was that the CD showed up on the desktop as the startup drive and your desktop background was funky.

Booting from Your System CD OS X

OS X: In Mac OS X you can also boot your Mac from the system CD. Actually, that's not entirely true. Well, it could be true. It depends on what you mean by true. You can boot your Mac from the Mac OS X Install CD but, unlike Mac OS 9, you can't access your drives and data files once it is booted up. What you *can* do is run First Aid and hope it can fix your problem so you can boot from your hard drive. To run First Aid, insert the Install CD into your drive, choose Restart from the Apple Menu, then hold down the letter C to force your Mac to boot from the CD rather than the hard drive. Once the Installer window opens, go to the menu bar at the top of the screen, click on Installer and select Open Disk Utility. Click on the First Aid tab, select your drive, click on Repair Disk and hope for the best.

Rebuilding the Desktop OS 9

OS 9: Back in Mac OS 9 when things started to get funky with your Mac, one of the first things you'd do was Rebuild the Desktop. In fact, if you called Apple Tech Support, usually the first thing they'd ask you was, "Did you rebuild the desktop?" (Followed by "Did you zap the PRAM?," followed by "Are you sure you actually own an Apple computer?") To rebuild the Desktop in Mac OS 9, you'd choose Restart from the Special menu, then as your Mac was restarting, just before the desktop appeared, you'd hold the Option and Command keys down. This would bring up a dialog asking "Are you sure you want to Rebuild the Desktop on Scott's Mac?" (I always thought this was pretty weird for people who weren't named Scott.) If you clicked OK, a status dialog would appear showing a sloth-like progress bar (it was actually more like a "no progress" bar) until the desktop was rebuilt.

Rebuilding the (Classic) Desktop OS X

OS X: Now, although there's no need to rebuild the desktop for Mac OS X, if you run any Classic environment applications (applications that haven't been updated to run under Mac OS X) you'll still need to Rebuild the Desktop for the Classic environment when problems arise. Luckily, it's easier to rebuild the Classic environment desktop than it was in Mac OS 9. Now, you simply go under the Apple menu, choose System Preferences, and in the resulting
dialog, click on the Classic Icon. When the Classic preferences appear, click on the Advanced tab, then under Other Classic Utilities, click on the Rebuild Desktop button. That's all there is to it.

Erasing and Reformatting a Drive OS 9

OS 9: To erase and format a drive in Mac OS 9 you opened the utility called Drive Setup, selected the drive you wanted to erase from a list of attached drives, chose a format, gave it a name, and clicked Erase.

Erasing and Reformatting a Drive OS X

OS X: Erasing a drive is pretty much the same in Mac OS X, except the utility you use is now called, imaginatively, Disk Utility. You'll find it in the Utilities folder inside the Applications folder. When you launch Disk Utilities, click on the Erase tab. Locate the drive you want to erase (it can be any drive except the one that is currently running Mac OS X) and click on it. Now look at the drive you've highlighted and make sure it's really the one you want to erase because if you erase the wrong one you are going to have a very bad day. Select the Volume Format from the pop-up menu, type in the name you want the drive to have, check one more time that you've selected the right drive (I'm not paranoid—really—just experienced), and click the Erase button. You will get a warning to let you know this is serious stuff and making sure you know what you're about to do. Click Erase and you're done.

Using Simple Finder OS 9

OS 9: In Mac OS 9, to turn on Simple Finder, you would go under the File menu, to Finder Preferences, then turn on Simple Finder.

Using Simple Finder OS X

OS X: Now, to set your Mac to display just the Simple Finder, go under the Apple menu and choose System Preferences, then click on the Account icon. When the Accounts preferences pane appears, click on your account, then click on the Capabilities button. When the Capabilites window opens, click on the Simple Finder button to turn on the Simple Finder function.

Restarting After a Crash OS 9

OS 9: In Mac OS 9, Macs actually crashed. I know, that's hard to believe, but it did happen from time to time. (Okay, it happened daily. Well, not daily, but at least weekly. Well, not for everybody, but for some people. Mean people mostly.) If things started acting wonky, or if one of your applications crashed (which basically meant you better restart soon before all hell breaks loose) you would restart by going under the Special Menu and choosing Restart. You could also use the keyboard shortcut Control-Command-Delete (which was especially helpful if your screen was frozen, and therefore you couldn't get to the Special menu).

Restarting After a Crash OS X

OS X: Now, you don't need Restart because OS X never, ever crashes. Okay, that's a bit of an exaggeration; actually now the system very rarely crashes. (I know some people using Mac OS X that have yet to have a System crash. I call these people "liars." Kidding.) Should you need to Restart, you'll now find it under the Apple menu (as shown above). On some Macs, you can also press the Power On button and that'll bring up a dialog where you can choose to Sleep, Shut Down, or Restart.

Using Apple's Built-in Help OS 9

OS 9: Back in Mac OS 9, you could access Apple's built-in Help function (called the Apple Help Viewer) by choosing Help from the Help Menu.

Using Apple's Built-in Help OS X

OS X: In Mac OS X, just choose Mac Help from the Help menu, or press Command-?. This brings up the new and improved Help Viewer (shown above). You can phrase questions like "What's the capital of Vermont?" (Or, if you actually want a chance of getting an answer, enter something more along the lines of "How do I Delete a file?" or "Where is the Trash Can?") When you click on the myriad answers it returns (sorted by possible relevance by default), a brief synopsis of the answer appears at the left bottom of the screen. If that sounds like the answer you're looking for, then double-click on it and a more complete answer appears.

Chapter Ten

X If you've bought a Mac in the last year
or so, it came with Mac OS X pre-installed,
so you skipped the whole terrifying Mac
OS X installation procedure. Now, is installing
Mac OS X really that scary? Not if you have the

Don't Freak Out
INSTALLING MAC OS X, AND OTHER SCARY STUFF

answers to the questions the Installer Assistant
will ask you. Here's the catch—you won't. Oh,
somebody, somewhere probably has the answers
(perhaps a high-ranking Apple employee or
Stephen Hawking) but not people like you and me.
So what's the best course of action when faced
with these questions? Guess. That's what I did,
and my Mac works just fine. Actually, I'm exag-
gerating (a bit). In fact, the installation process is
surprisingly simple if you're an Apple authorized
service tech. See, I'm kidding—you fell for it again.
Honestly, it is a breeze, but there are a couple of
questions it will ask you that might freak you out.
Primarily because you have to give your answers
in Portuguese, and spelling counts. Again, just a
joke. Besides the things that might freak you out
during installation (few though they may be), there
are a couple of other things that might make you
spaz so I covered those too. (By the way, the term
"spaz" is actually derived from the Portuguese
word "spazzulita" which loosely translated means
"one who has installed Mac OS X but cannot speak
Portuguese and therefore cannot answer critical
installation questions.")

1. Do I Really Need All this Stuff?

If you install everything that is included on your Mac OS X Install CDs, you will likely fill more drive space than the combined capacity of the first five hard drives you owned—it's huge. Here are some of the options you'll have when you install to help you sort out what you need and what you can leave on the CD.

Don't Need: *This gives you the option to set-up your System's Localized Files using other languages (Dansk, Nederlands, Suomi, Deutsch). Saves 240 MB.*

Don't Need: *Unless you want your System to use an Asian language. Saves 155 MB.*

Don't Need: *You should have the drivers for your existing printers already installed, unless you just want a gazillion drivers on your system you'll probably never use. Saves 500MB.*

Don't Need if: *You don't want "iApps" such as iTunes, iChat, iPhoto, etc. Saves 180 MB.*

Need if: *You want to network your computer, access the Internet, and want Mac OS X to run well. If you feel lucky, you can save 132 MB.*

2. Where's All the Stuff I Had on My Desktop?

In a recent poll of persons planning on upgrading to Mac OS X, when asked their greatest fear about the upgrade, 50% responded, "I'm afraid I'm going to lose some important stuff." (I won't tell you what the other person said—suffice it to say they need therapy.)

When you see the beautiful aqua Desktop for the first time you will not see all the folders and icons you had so neatly arranged on your desktop in Mac OS 9. Don't freak out—all your stuff is safe; it's just moved to a folder called, "Desktop (Mac OS 9)." All of your old applications are still there, too, in a folder named, "Applications (Mac OS 9)."

OS X: You've heard the horror stories. You've read the comments of people in the forums who were one page away from finishing their doctoral dissertation when they installed Mac OS X and started sobbing uncontrollably as they booted up their Mac and their work of the past three years wasn't on the desktop where they left it. They can deal with the dissertation—it's their extensive collection of bookmarks to Klingon and Cardacian language discussion forums that has them upset. You won't lose a thing when you upgrade to Mac OS X—files, applications, e-mails, bookmarks—they're all safe.

3. Why is Mac OS 9 Opening?

OS X: If you launch an application, and something that looks like Mac OS 9 starts opening in a new window on the desktop, don't freak out. It's just Mac OS 9 opening in a new
window on the desktop. While Mac OS X is the latest, greatest operating system available
on the planet, there are still some applications which haven't yet been rewritten to be able
to run in it. When you open a document created with one of these applications (officially
known as Classic applications, but commonly called Lame applications) Mac OS X opens
the Classic environment and runs the application with Mac OS 9. There is another group of
applications (known as Carbon applications) that can run in *both* Mac OS X and the Classic
environment. If you have one of those applications, and want to run it in Classic (I don't
know why you would, but it's certainly possible that somewhere, someone might) you can
click on the application, press Command-I, then in the Info palette, click on the checkbox
for "Open in the Classic environment." The third group consists of applications written to
take full advantage of Mac OS X's power, a.k.a. Native or Cocoa applications.

4. I'm Sorry, Dave. I'm Afraid I Can't Let You Do That.

OS X: One thing that freaks people out in Mac OS X is the area of permission. The first time you run across it will probably be when you go to install an application, and before it will let you, it asks you to enter your administrator password so it can make sure you're actually allowed to install a program on this machine. It gets even uglier when you attempt to drag a file into or out of a folder or to the Trash and you get a warning that there is no way you are going to be allowed to move that file. There are several reasons why you get such warnings. It might be as simple as "the file is locked" to prevent accidental erasure; or it could be that whoever owns the file doesn't want you messing with it. If you're on a network, the system administrator may not have given you full privileges. So how do you get around this? If you're trying to delete something go ask your Administrator (and don't forget to say please) if they'll let you toss something in the Trash. If you're trying to install something, ask the administrator either to install it or to share their password—which is pretty unlikely because then they lose their "God-like" control over your Mac.

5. You're Locked Out of a Preference

OS X: If you don't know what you're doing and engage in casual clicking, dragging, and deleting, it's possible to really mess up your Mac. Mac OS X allows anyone who is an administrator to lock certain Preference panes to keep users from messing with them, which can prevent some major headaches. Two groups of people put this feature to good use: parents and Network Administrators. How to you get around this? Parents—don't bother trying. Network Administrators—take them out for drinks, get 'em hammered, and then ask them to give you the password. This works at least six to seven times out of ten.

6. There's More Than One Library Folder

Macintosh HD — Library

Macintosh HD — System — Library

Macintosh HD — Users — felixnel — Library

OS X: Libraries can be confusing to people moving from Mac OS 9 to Mac OS X for two reasons: First, there were none in Mac OS 9 and, secondly, there are at least three of them in Mac OS X. The reason for and functioning of the multiple Libraries is linked directly to Mac OS X's multi-user environment. In Mac OS 9, the "behind the scenes" functions of your Mac were handled by Control Panels, Extensions, and other items in the System folder. In Mac OS X, the files that "run" your Mac are located in Libraries. Items needed for all users (fonts, applications, etc.) are in the main Library and can be accessed by anyone with an account. Items that can only be accessed by an administrator are kept in the Library within the System folder. Finally, every user has a Library, accessible only to them, containing files necessary for creating their desktop, preference settings, etc. So if you are looking for your browser bookmark file, for example, you would look in the Preference file within your user Library. If you want to add a desktop picture that can be used by anyone with an account on your Mac, you would put it in the main Library.

7. My Fonts are Everywhere!

OS X: The first time you start clicking your way around your hard drive after installing Mac OS X, I guarantee you'll think it's déjà vu because it will seem that everywhere you turn you're running into a fonts folder. There are a lot of places you can store fonts in Mac OS X depending on whom you want to be able to access them. One thing you don't want to do is mess with the fonts folder that is within the Library folder, within the System folder. You might never even have known about this folder since it's buried so deep, but now that I've told you about it you're tempted to go and mess with it, aren't you? Don't do it. Bad things can happen. If fonts are freaking you out, go to Chapter 6, "Fonts and Printing," for more information.

8. Disk Images and Packages

When you download an application, it usually arrives compressed. Sometimes this process (from compressed file to mounted disk) happens automatically, but sometimes you'll have to click an icon.

When you Click on the mounted drive image on your desktop, you will see the application installer, often a package.

OS X: Mac OS X often uses disk images as part of the installation process for an application. They can freak you out a bit the first time because, well . . . they're different. You run across them mostly when you download an application from the Web and you go to your desktop looking for the application you just downloaded and instead find three files with very similar names (you don't always see three—sometimes it's only two) including one that ends with the suffix .dmg. Mac users have had the ability to create disk images (.dmg files) with Disk Copy for some time, but Mac OS X is the first operating system to use them widely. Packages, on the other hand, are new to Mac OS X. They are essentially a special type of folder that holds an application and all its support files. But unlike the application folders you are accustomed to in Mac OS 9, clicking on a package doesn't open a window showing the application file along with all the supports; it simply launches the application.

9. Where's The Chooser?

OS X: In Mac OS 9, if you wanted to select a printer or log into a network you went to the Chooser. In Mac OS X, the Chooser is gone. Instead, you now choose your printer directly from the Print dialog of the application you're printing from, saving untold confusion. Chapter Six has more on selecting printers. Logging into networks is easier, too—now you can access a network from the menu bar of any Finder window (see Chapter 7, "Networking and the Internet").

10. Optimizing System Performance

OS X: This one is guaranteed to drive you crazy. It happens after you install some applications. (If it happened every time, for all applications, then it wouldn't be confusing. The only pattern I've been able to figure out is that it usually occurs when you are in a hurry. Like when the flight attendant announces that the plane can't take off until the passenger in 19C turns off their laptop. All you were doing was installing a game to play on the flight. It's almost as if your Mac detects you are in a hurry [kind of like dogs sensing fear] because the bigger the hurry, the longer the optimization process takes.) It really does serve a vital purpose, but I won't bore you with the technical details, even though I really do know them. I just wanted to let you know about it so you won't freak out when it happens.

Chapter Eleven

9 I know what you're thinking—there are only 20 cool things? Of course not, there are loads of things you can do in Mac OS X that you couldn't do in Mac OS 9, but some of them are: (a) automatic, (b) too big to be called little things,

20 Cool Little Things You Couldn't Do in Mac OS 9

(like preemptive multitasking, protected memory, etc.), and (c) I can't think of a "c" right now. Some things are actually fairly major, but those features didn't make it into Apple's ads—like the new Finder Window toolbar. It's pretty darn handy, and chances are you'll be using it every day, but it doesn't get the press like "preemptive multitasking" does. Why does preemptive multitasking get all the press? It's simple. Preemptive multitasking has hired its own Washington-based lobbyists, and an L.A.-based PR firm to make sure it stays in the public eye. How do you think you all those photos of J-Lo and Preemptive Multitasking dining at a trendy Hollywood bistro got on the cover of the *Enquirer*? You think some Hollywood reporter just happened to be dining at (insert Hollywood bistro name here), looked up, saw J-Lo and PM (that's his street name) and started snapping shots with his D-100? Not bloody likely. Those were set-ups. Mini-events concocted by the PR firms to make it look like PM is a player, that he's "out there" and making some noise. In reality, PM spends most nights alone, in front of the TV, with a cheap bottle of wine and take-out fajitas from Chili's.

1. iStuff OS X

OS X: In Mac OS 9, you had a couple of "i" programs: iMovie and iTunes. Both great programs, mind you, but after the success of those two, Apple starting introducing more wonderful iStuff, exclusively for Mac OS X. These new "Digital Hub" apps include: iPhoto (an absolutely amazing application for sorting, viewing, printing, and organizing your digital photos); iChat (a way cool chat application); iCal (probably the most ingenious computer-based calendar ever); and iSync (for syncing your Mac and your iPod or handheld Palm-like device). Also, all the new and improved versions of iMovie and iTunes are available ONLY to OS X users—another reason you'll be glad you switched.

2. Drag Items to the Dock OS X

OS X: You couldn't just drag things to the Apple menu back in Mac OS 9, but in Mac OS X you can drag items right into the Dock (which replaced the Apple Menu) by just clicking on a file and dragging it to the Dock. If it's an application, drag it to the left side of the Dock's divider line. If it's a folder, a file, etc., drag it to the right side.

3. Automatically Download Digital Photos OS X

OS X: Getting digital photos into Mac OS 9 was a major pain, because there was nothing built-in to do the job. But in Mac OS X, just hook up your digital camera, or plug in
a memory card from your digital camera, and a dialog opens, asking if you want to use
iPhoto, Image Capture, or some other application as your default application for handling
digital photos. The next time you hook up a camera or insert a media card, the application
you selected as your default will automatically open and download your photos. Ahh, life
is sweet.

4. Control Music Playing in the Background OS X

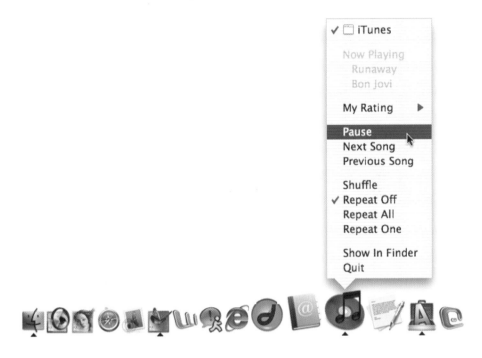

OS X: If you were playing a song with iTunes in OS 9, and you wanted to do anything—change songs, pause a song, repeat it, etc., you had to leave the program you were in, switch to iTunes, and then you could make your adjustments. But in OS X, you're just one click away, without leaving your current application. Control-click on the iTunes icon in the Dock and up pops a menu where you can control any songs you have playing (as shown above).

5. Keep Working with an Open Dialog OS X

OS X: This is something that doesn't sound like much, until you use it the first time and realize what a pain it was to not have this feature in previous operating systems. In Mac OS X you have the ability to ignore alert boxes and warning dialogs until such time as you want to deal with them. In Mac OS 9 when one of these babies appeared on screen, everything stopped until you dealt with it. No more. Now you can even click out of a print dialog to check on something. It will sit in the background waiting for you to get back to it. The next time you are installing a new application and it asks for a serial number, no more having to cancel the installation process to go look in the folder where you carefully stored it, write it down, and start the install again. Now you can simply let your install box wait while you retrieve the information. The first time you do this you may not even realize what you've done, but at some point it will hit you and you'll wonder how you ever put up with the old way.

6. Add Items to a Window's Toolbar OS X

OS X: In Mac OS 9 there just wasn't a window toolbar (like the one shown above, just below the title bar), so adding items to the non-existent toolbar was pretty much out of the question. Now, you can add folders, files, and even applications to this handy bar by just dragging them up there.

7. Force Quit Without Crashing OS X

OS X: Every once in a while, Mac OS 9 would let you try to Force Quit a frozen application. It only allowed this once in a while, because it was usually so busy trying to crash your entire Mac it really didn't care about anything else. It was usually pretty successful in crashing or freezing your whole system; so getting the opportunity to actually Force Quit in Mac OS 9 was a cause of great celebration, because you might, just might, have enough time to save open documents in other applications. Luckily, in Mac OS X, if an Application freezes (hey, it happens once in a while), you can safely Force Quit (using the dialog shown above) and go on about your business. You can relaunch the frozen application or go and do something else—it doesn't matter, it doesn't "bring down" your Mac. To Force Quit a running application, just go under the Apple Menu and choose Force Quit to bring up the dialog shown above, click on the name of the application you want to quit, then press the Force Quit button.

8. Mail and Address Book OS X

OS X: Apple included two new applications with Mac OS X that are just wonderful: Mail and Address Book, and they have built-in interconnectivity (I'm not even sure what that word means) that can really boost your productivity (and just generally make your life easier). The two applications are simple in their design, yet elegant in their use, and once you start using them you'll never look back.

9. Make a PDF from Any Application OS X

OS X: If you can print a document, you can create a PDF of it which anyone with Adobe Reader (previously called Acrobat Reader and available free from Adobe) can view regardless of computer platform. Open the document you want to convert to a PDF, press Command-P to open the print dialog, and click the Save As PDF button in the lower left of the dialog. Give the file a name and a destination and you're done.

10. Resizing Icons in Icon View OS X

OS X: You didn't have much control over the size of icons when you viewed a window in Icon view back in Mac OS 9. But if you want big icons in Mac OS X, you got 'em. Just open a Finder window, then press Command-J to bring up the View preferences (as shown above). Then drag the Icon Size slider to the right to make them larger, to the left to make them smaller (as shown). You can also choose to have this apply to all windows or just to this one by selecting one of the options at the top of the dialog.

11. Previewing Movies and Audio in Column View OS X

OS X: Now if you have a QuickTime video clip, or an audio file, you can get a live preview of the contents of that file, as long as you're in Column View (as shown above). Just click on the movie or audio clip, and the QuickTime window will appear enabling you to preview the clip right within the window, rather than having to launch the QuickTime player.

12. Skip the Shutdown Warning OS X

OS X: For as long as I can remember, when you went to Shut Down your Mac, it tried to talk you out of it, with an "Are you sure?" dialog similar to the one above (top). Luckily, in OS X you can bypass this warning by simply holding the Option key before you choose Shut Down. By doing this, you skip the annoying question and your Mac just shuts right down. With the Pro Keyboard, pressing Control-Eject brings up the dialog with four buttons shown above (bottom). This is a quick, convenient way to restart or sleep your Mac either by clicking a button or by pressing the R or S key.

13. Name Files with More than 31 Characters OS X

Really, you can name this file pretty much anything you want, and the name field will just keep expanding. Not bad, eh?

OS X: The maxium file name length of 31 characters has been lifted, and you've got the OK to start going crazy by naming files with up to 256 characters. Just click on a file, start typing, and long names will automatically wrap to the next line. Warning:This is a dangerous tip because if you do not use restraint you are going to make people very angry if you start e-mailing them files that have entire paragraphs for file names. Like many things in life—just because you can doesn't mean you necessarily should.

14. See Folder/File Info in Icon View OS X

OS X: Now, if you want to know how many items are in a folder, you can turn on Show Item Info (by opening a window, pressing Command-J, and turning on Show item info as shown above), and (when viewed in Icon view) the number of items in a folder will appear just below each folder (as shown above). Another cool thing is that QuickTime movie icons (when viewed in this fashion) will display their running length.

15. Seeing Your Filename Extensions OS X

OS X: Although Macs don't need filename extensions like some, shall we say, less desirable computer platforms, if you are going to be exchanging files with persons who have not yet moved up to the Mac they are a necessity. Mac OS X gives you the option of seeing your filenames displayed with or without the extension. To set your preference, from the Finder, go to the menu bar, select Finder and choose Preferences. At the bottom of the dialog that opens you will see a checkbox you can select if you want the filename extensions to be visible.

16. Viewing Windows in Column View OS X

OS X: There's a new way to view and navigate your Finder Windows in Mac OS X, and that's Column view (shown above). This lets you quickly scroll to the right, expanding folders as you go, to get to your desired files, rather than having to open folder after folder. I know people who love this new Column view with every fiber of their being, and although I agree it's a wonderful new addition to Mac OS X, I still can't help but be worried about these people, at least on some level.

17. Seeing Thumbnail Previews of Icons OS X

OS X: In Mac OS 9, if your photos didn't have thumbnail icon previews, you saw generic icons instead (and incidentally, most Digital Camera photos use the generic JPEG icon). But in Mac OS X, if you turn on Show icon preview it will automatically replace these generic icons with full color preview icons picturing the images (as shown above). To turn this feature on, open a window, then press Command-J to open the View Preferences, then turn on the Show icon preview checkbox (as shown).

18. Add Menu Bar Controls OS X

OS X: The Control Strip from Mac OS 9 is a thing of the past. It's been replaced with something much less intrusive, and much more convenient—menu bar items. The checkboxes to turn on individual menu bar items are found in the System Preferences for specific features (e.g., to turn on the Sound menu bar item, go to the Sound System Preferences). Now you can access things like your System Volume, Monitor Depth and Resolution, AirPort, and Modem controls directly from the top right side of your menu bar. Just click on the menu item and a drop-down menu appears (as shown).

19. Built-in Two-Button Mouse Support OS X

OS X: Even though Apple still doesn't offer a two-button mouse, Mac OS X supports the use of one. By default the second (right-click) button is set to perform the same functions as the Mac's Control key, and support is also built in for the scroll wheel found on many two-button mice.

20. Lock Access to Preferences OS X

OS X: If you have put a particular System Preference in place and you don't want some goober messing around with your settings, you can lock these preferences to prevent further changes by clicking on the Lock icon in the bottom left-hand corner of key System Preference panes (as shown above). This means of course, that if you later decide to make changes, you'll need to use your Administrator User password to unlock the preferences.

Chapter Twelve

Are there really things you could do back in Mac OS 9 that you can't do using today's new and improved Mac OS X? Sadly yes. Not many, mind you, but a few. These are the things we don't talk about at Mac parties (OK, they're not

20 Little Things Apple Changed Just to Mess with Your Head

ACTUALLY, THERE'S A METHOD BEHIND THEIR MADNESS. AT LEAST THAT'S WHAT WE'VE BEEN LED TO BELIEVE.

really parties, they're more like loosely organized self-help meetings with group therapy overtones.) But more than looking at how your #1 all-time favorite feature from Mac OS 9 didn't make the trip over to Mac OS X, instead this chapter looks at things you don't need to do anymore. You see, there were things—horrible, unspeakable things, that you used to have to do that you just don't have to anymore. One thing that's gone is the constant praying. Mac OS 9 users spent a part of each day silently praying that the application they were running wouldn't freeze, because they knew that if it did, it would bring down their entire machine. There are lots of good reasons to pray (Lotto being one), but wasting good quality prayers on having your Mac OS not crash was counter-productive (especially since God has His hands full with prayer requests from Windows users, which apparently start before the average Windows user even boots their machine, and continues for hours after they've shut down). So this chapter is really lots of good news, sprinkled with tiny particles of bad news (namely numbers 2, 3, 8, 11, 12, and 17). Okay, maybe 18 and 20 too.

1. Put Away Is Gone, Undo Is Here

OS X: In Mac OS 9, if you moved a file out of a folder, you could usually click on that file, press Command-Y (the shortcut for the Put Away command), and that file would jump back to its original folder. This was particularly helpful when you dragged something into the Trash, and then changed your mind—Command-Y would put the selected file back where it came from. In Mac OS X, this command has been replaced and expanded by Undo. Whereas Put Away just put stuff away, Undo reverses most Finder functions. For example, if you carefully sort through a folder of digital photos, selecting the ones you want to move to a new folder then drag them to the wrong folder, press Command-Z and they all go back into the original folder (still selected) where you can grab them again and put them in the right folder. Or if you highlight an icon, change the name, then change your mind, Undo will change it back (Put Away would be of no help).

2. No Window Shade: Minimize Instead

OS X: Mac OS 9's Window Shade feature (the ability to double-click on the title bar of an open Finder window and have it roll up like a window shade, leaving just the title bar still visible) is gone. In Mac OS X when you double-click an open window, instead of "rolling up" it minimizes to the Dock. In some ways this is better than the old Window Shade feature because it removes the window from the desktop area altogether, making things less cluttered than in Mac OS 9.

3. Scrapbook Is Long Gone

OS X: In Mac OS 9, you could copy and paste low-resolution graphics into a Scrapbook Utility. Then, if you needed to use one of these low-res graphics, you could open the Scrapbook, scroll to the desired graphic, copy it, and paste it into an open application. Since the Scrapbook only supported low-resolution graphics, it was of little use, so in Mac OS X it's gone, and it really hasn't been replaced by anything. In short, "She's gone-on-on-on-on, oh-oh-oh-I-I, I better learn to how to face it...."

4. There's No Trash Can on the Desktop

OS X: The famous Macintosh Trash can no longer lives on the desktop (as it did in all previous versions of the Mac OS), it's now located at the far right end of the Dock. What if you don't want it at the far right end of the Dock? Tough. That's where they put it and that's where it stays. Try to move it—go ahead. Just can't play by the rules, can you? Always have to push the envelope a bit (that's why you're a Mac user).

5. The Special Menu Is Gone

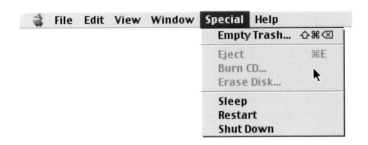

OS X: The Special Menu in Mac OS 9 held a number of commands like Shut Down, Erase, Eject, and Restart. The Special Menu is gone in Mac OS X and these commands have, for the most part, moved under the Apple Menu. See Chapter 8, "Other Stuff," for how to shut down, eject a disk, erase a file, and restart you computer.

6. SimpleText Is Now TextEdit

OS X: Remember SimpleText? It was a great little program. It launched faster than a greased pig, and although it lacked a few key things (like a spell checker) it was pretty handy for a quick note. Well, in Mac OS X it's been replaced by TextEdit, which still launches as fast as an oily squealer (with no splash screen to slow things down). TextEdit has lots of word processor-like features, such as enhanced control of fonts, type tweaking, and other useful functions. TextEdit is also Mac OS X-native, which means that it offers features such as Services, font preview, and special characters not available before.

7. Virtual Memory Is Virtually Gone

OS X: Back in Mac OS 9, you could set aside a chunk of your empty hard drive space to be used as Virtual Memory—a slower form of RAM. Depending on what you used your Mac for, Virtual Memory could slow down your applications (especially applications like Photoshop), but otherwise it was cheaper than buying real RAM. Well, in Mac OS X, Virtual Memory has been replaced by an entirely new, more efficient memory scheme which operates automatically; so the Memory Control Panel, used in Mac OS 9 to turn Virtual Memory on/off, is now long gone.

8. Control Strip Is Replaced by Menu Items

OS X: If you liked Mac OS 9's Control Strip, you'll love Mac OS X's Menu Items, which add many of the Control Strip's functions right to the menu bar. This makes your desktop less cluttered (because they're not visible in your work area); and they're always there (they don't have to be opened and closed to be used).

9. Application Folders Are Nearly Gone

Control-click on a Package's icon and choose See Package Contents from the contextual menu and a new window will open showing all the associated files.

OS X: In Mac OS 9, when you installed an application, the support files for the application (sometimes ten or more with cryptic names that disclosed nothing about their function) were typically stored along with the application in a folder. You always had the suspicion that you didn't need all of them, but you also feared if you trashed one it would be the one support file you did need. In Mac OS X, many applications are installed as what is called a "package." The support files are still there, but all you see on your desktop is one icon. If you want to see the support files you can Control-click on this icon and select See Package Contents from the pop-up menu. But when you want to open the application, instead of having to sift through a long list of files to find the actual application file, you just click on the package's icon. Another handy thing about packages is that there's now little chance of users accidentally throwing away important support files for their applications.

10. The Launcher Is Replaced by the Dock

OS X: The Launcher in Mac OS 9 let you drag your commonly used applications, folders, and files to a floating palette that gave you one-click access to them. The Launcher of old has been replaced by the Dock, which does exactly the same thing in a much more elegant way. (See Chapter 1, "The Apple Menu," to learn how to move applications and files to the Dock for one-click launching.)

11. No SimpleSound for Recording Audio

OS X: Here's one you might miss: Mac OS 9 came with an application called SimpleSound, which let users with a built-in or external mic record audio clips that were as long as their available hard drive space would allow. So if you wanted to record your ramblings for 30 minutes, that wasn't a problem (well, your friends and family might take issue, but not the OS). In Mac OS X, although you can record your own Alert sounds, the SimpleSound application is gone and hasn't been replaced. Goodbye SimpleSound, goodbye, my friend.

12. The Print Window Command Is Gone

OS X: Here's another one you might miss from Mac OS 9. Back then, you could print any open Finder window by going under the File menu and choosing Print Window. If you didn't have any windows open, you could print the desktop. Sadly, this feature didn't make its way into Mac OS X, but as a workaround you can take a screen capture of the window (Shift-Command-4-Spacebar, then click on the window), placing a PDF file on your desktop. Double-click the PDF to open in Preview, and you can print the screen capture. The problem is, a screen capture only contains what's visible on screen, so if you have a window with more content than can be shown on screen, you'll have to take one screen capture, scroll down, take another, and so forth. It's not pretty, it's not fun, but it works.

13. No Need to Rebuild the Desktop

OS X: In Mac OS 9, rebuilding the desktop was almost a weekly event (if you didn't rebuild it weekly, you probably should have). Well, Mac OS X itself needs no rebuilding of the desktop so that's just one more thing you don't have to worry about. However, if you're using Mac OS X's Classic environment to run Mac OS 9-only applications (applications that haven't yet been updated to run in Mac OS X), you'll still have to rebuild the desktop from time to time if things in Classic mode start acting weird (icons start messing up, etc.). But luckily, even if you have to rebuild the desktop in Mac OS 9, even that's easier in Mac OS X. See Chapter 9, "Troubleshooting," for how to rebuild Classic's desktop.

14. No Need for Adobe Type Manager (ATM)

OS X: In Mac OS 9, for PostScript Type 1 fonts to look smooth on screen (especially at large point sizes), you had to have a separate Control Panel utility from Adobe called Adobe Type Manager (ATM) installed on your Mac. It was a "miracle utility" and it did an amazingly great job. As great as ATM was, Mac OS X doesn't need it because of its built-in font smoothing technology. If you're using old applications (ones that have to run in Classic environment because they haven't yet been updated for Mac OS X), then you'll still need to install ATM into your Classic system.

15. No Need to Manage Extensions

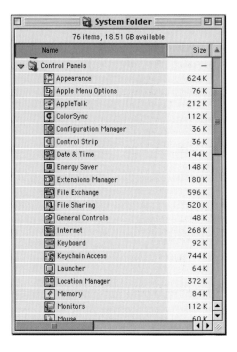

OS X: Back in Mac OS 9, you would customize your system by dropping all sorts of different Extensions and Control Panels into your System Folder. Which Extensions and Control Panels actually loaded into your system, and their loading order, was controlled by Extensions Manager. Since you no longer drop things into your System Folder in Mac OS X, the need to manage extensions is gone, as is the Extensions Manager.

16. No More Chooser for Choosing Printers

OS X: In Mac OS 9, you had to let your Mac know which printer you wanted to use by designating it in the Chooser. In Mac OS X, the Chooser is gone. Instead, you now choose your printer directly from the Print dialog of the application you're printing from, saving untold confusion and doing away with the need for a Chooser. (See Chapter 6, "Fonts and Printing," for more on printing in Mac OS X.)

17. Finder Button View Is Replaced by Dock

OS X: In Mac OS 9, there was a window mode (along with List View and Icon View) called Button view, that turned your icons into large buttons for one-click access. This feature is gone in Mac OS X, as the Dock now pretty much handles one-click access to applications and files. However, some people will miss this view. People who like huge buttons. I call these "Huge-button-lovers." No, it's not a very creative name, but that's all I've got. Of course, Huge-Button-Lovers can make their Mac OS X icons huge in View Options, but they'll only be huge icons, not Buttons.

18. No Drag and Drop Desktop Printing

OS X: In Mac OS 9, you could put icons of connected printers right on your desktop, and if you wanted to print a file, you could just drag and drop it right on the printer icon of your choice. In Mac OS X, this ability is gone. Gone, gone, gone. However, if you add Print Center to your Dock, you can get the same result.

19. The Application Menu Is Now the Dock

Internet Explorer

OS X: In Mac OS 9 you used to switch between open applications by going to the Application menu in the upper right-hand corner of the menu bar and you'd choose an active application to switch to from the pop-down list. In Mac OS X, application switching is handled (like about everything else) by the Dock. You can switch to any running application by simply clicking on its icon in the Dock. *Note:* You can also step through open applications using the keyboard shortcut Command-Tab.

20. Color Coding (Finder Labels) Are Gone

OS X: In Mac OS 9, you could color code Finder icons and folders for easy visual identification. This is gone in Mac OS X, and there's no built-in way to color code files. However, although this doesn't really replace color coding, Apple wants you to think it does, so I'll include it—rather than color coding files for easy identification, you can add a comment (in the Comments field of the Info window) and these comments can be viewed in a Finder Window set to List View.

Index

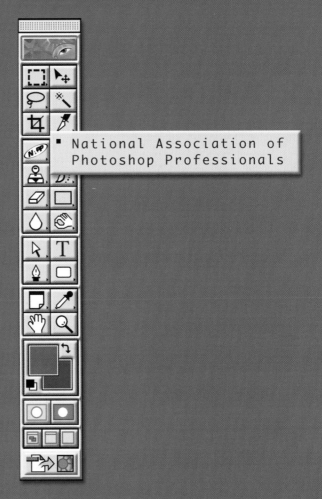

National Association of
Photoshop Professionals

The only tool you need to master Adobe Photoshop

If you use Photoshop, you know that it's never been more important to stay up to date with your Photoshop skills as it is today. That's what the National Association of Photoshop Professionals (NAPP) is all about, as we're the world's leading resource for Photoshop training, education, and news. If you're into Photoshop, you're invited to join our worldwide community of Photoshop users from 106 different countries around the world who share their ideas, solutions, and cutting-edge techniques. Join NAPP today—it's the right tool for the job.

Hey Scott, I just upgraded to OS X. How Do I...?

If you've recently upgraded to Mac OS X, chances are you've got plenty of questions. Luckily, now you can get the answers you need fast with *Kelby's Notes for Mac OS X*, a new Help menu that puts the answers just one click away.

Here's how it works: the Kelby's Notes for Mac OS X plug-in adds a new menu to the Finder's Menu bar called **How Do I?** Anytime you're stuck, just go right to this new menu, and you'll find a list of the top 100 most-asked Mac OS X questions. Choose the one you need, and a dialog box pops up showing a screen capture and simple, plain-English instructions on how to do it (as shown below). There's no faster, easier way to get the help you need. Order yours today.

Kelby's Notes works with Mac OS X, version 10.0 or higher.

ADDITIONAL RESOURCES

ScottKelbyBooks.com
For information on Scott's other Macintosh and graphics-related books, visit his book site. For background info on Scott, visit www.scottkelby.com.

http://www.scottkelbybooks.com

Mac Design Magazine
Scott is Editor-in-Chief of *Mac Design Magazine,* "The Graphics Magazine for Macintosh Users." It's a tutorial-based print magazine with how-to columns on Photoshop, Illustrator, QuarkXPress, Dreamweaver, GoLive, Flash, Final Cut Pro, and more. It's also packed with tips, tricks, and shortcuts for your favorite graphics applications.

http://www.macdesignonline.com

National Association of Photoshop Professionals (NAPP)
The industry trade association for Adobe® Photoshop® users and the world's leading resource for Photoshop training, education, and news.

http://www.photoshopuser.com

KW Computer Training Videos
Scott Kelby is featured in a series of more than 20 Photoshop training videos, each on a particular Photoshop topic, available from KW Computer Training. Visit the Web site or call 813-433-5000 for orders or more information.

http://www.photoshopvideos.com

Photoshop 7 Down & Dirty Tricks
Scott is also author of the best-selling book *Photoshop 7 Down & Dirty Tricks,* and the book's companion Web site has all the info on the book, which is available at bookstores around the country.

http://www.downanddirtytricks.com

Adobe Photoshop Seminar Tour
See Scott live at the Adobe Photoshop Seminar Tour, the nation's most popular Photoshop seminars. For upcoming tour dates and class schedules, visit the tour Web site.

http://www.photoshopseminars.com

PhotoshopWorld
The convention for Adobe Photoshop users has now become the largest Photoshop-only event in the world. Scott Kelby is technical chair and education director for the event, as well as one of the instructors.

http://www.photoshopworld.com

Photoshop Photo-Retouching Secrets
Scott is also the author of *Photoshop Photo-Retouching Secrets.* The book's companion Web site has all the info on the book and features downloadable source files for many of the projects. The book is available at bookstores around the country.

http://www.photoretouchingsecrets.com

Photoshop Hall of Fame
Created to honor and recognize those individuals whose contributions to the art and business of Adobe Photoshop have had a major impact on the application or the Photoshop community itself.

http://www.photoshophalloffame.com

The Ultimate Collection of Mac OS X Sidebar Tips (Without the Sidebars)

Mac OS X v. 10.2 Jaguar Killer Tips
By Scott Kelby

Getting Rid of the Preview Column

If you've used Mac OS X's Column View, you know that when you click on a file, you'll get a large preview of that file in a new column type called "The Preview Column." Click on a graphic—you see its preview. Large! This "feature" annoys the heck out of some people (you know who you are), so to turn off this special column, just view a window in Column View, then press Command-J to bring up the Column View Options. Turn off the checkbox for "Show Preview column" and this wonderful (yet occasionally annoying) preview column will disappear.

Keep a Running App in the Dock After You Quit

If you're running an application and you say to yourself, "You know, I use this app a lot," you can keep its icon in the Dock, even after you've quit the app, so next time it's just one click away. Just Control-click on the app's icon in the Dock, and choose "Keep in Dock." Of course, there is another way. A cooler way. An "I don't need no stinkin' pop-up menu" way. Just click on the running application's icon, drag it away from the Dock, pause a second, and then drag it right back. It's really no faster, but it makes you look (and feel) less pop-up menu co-dependent.

Turn on the Crash Early Warning System

This tip is bordering on geek-dom, so before you use it, it wouldn't hurt to grab the nearest pocket protector before you read any further. If you crash, you can ask Mac OS X to let you know why you crashed (but you have to turn this feature on before the crash—it's turned off by default). Perhaps more important than that, if this feature is turned on, it may pop up and warn you that something's wrong, just before you crash—giving you just enough time to save your open documents. To turn this "crash early-warning system" on, look inside your hard drive, inside your Utilities folder, and launch an application called "Console." From the Console menu, choose "Preferences," and in the Preferences panel click on the Crashes tab. Then, click on the checkboxes for "Enable crash reporting" and "Automatically display crash logs." If you crash (or in some cases if you're about to crash), a window will appear with a log of what's happened, or what's about to happen. That's your cue.

The Hottest Collection of Cool Tips and Hidden Secrets

Photoshop 7 Killer Tips
By Scott Kelby and Felix Nelson

Tweak All Your Type With One Fell Swoop!

This is a pretty darn slick tip for changing the font, size, or color of a number of different Type layers all at once. Here's how it's done: First, link all the layers that you want to adjust by clicking in the second column beside each Type layer. Once all the layers are linked, hold the Shift key and make your change. The change you make to one Type layer will also affect all the linked Type layers. The key is not to highlight your type. Just choose the Type tool and go straight to the Options Bar or the Character palette. Schweeeet!

New Document Timesaver

This is a *huge* timesaver, and once you start using it, you'll use it almost every day. It enables you to create a new document that automatically matches the exact dimensions, color mode, and resolution of any other document that you already have open. Here's how: Go under the File menu and choose New. When the New document dialog box opens, go under the Window menu, under Documents, and you'll see a list of all your open documents at the bottom of the menu. Choose the document you want to emulate, and its size, color mode, and resolution will instantly be entered into your New document dialog box—all you have to do is click OK, and a new document with those specs will appear. This one may sound a bit lightweight, until you try it a couple of times.

WWW.PEACHPIT.COM

Quality How-to Computer Books

About

News

Books

Features

Resources

Order

Find

Welcome!

Visit Peachpit Press on the Web at www.peachpit.com

- Check out new feature articles each Monday: excerpts, interviews, tips, and plenty of how-tos

- Find any Peachpit book by title, series, author, or topic on the Books page

- See what our authors are up to on the News page: signings, chats, appearances, and more

- Meet the Peachpit staff and authors in the About section: bios, profiles, and candid shots

- Use Resources to reach our academic, sales, customer service, and tech support areas and find out how to become a Peachpit author

Peachpit.com is also the place to:

- Chat with our authors online
- Take advantage of special Web-only offers
- Get the latest info on new books

Top Ten Troubleshooting Tips for Jaguar

When Apple upgraded Mac OS X to 10.2 (Jaguar), it didn't forget troubleshooters. Among the many new features in Jaguar are ones that are especially useful for solving problems. Here are 10 of my favorites:

Mac OS X Disaster Relief,
Updated Edition By Ted Landau

1. Do a clean install

If your Mac OS X software ever gets sufficiently messed up that you want to start over and reinstall it, Jaguar gives you a new way to do this. It's especially useful if you have already installed 10.2.1 or later, and want to start over again by first downgrading to 10.2. In previous versions of Mac OS X, Apple insisted that doing a downgrade required that you first erase the drive entirely. Not so in Jaguar. Instead, you start-up from the Mac OS X 10.2 Install CD and select the Archive and Install option via the Options button in the Installer's Select Destination window. You'll also want to select the Preserve Users and Network Settings sub-option. The Installer will place a fresh copy of 10.2 on your drive but still preserve most of the custom changes and additions you have made. All the old software is moved to a new folder called Previous Systems, just in case there are files there that you may still want to use.

One hitch: If you have the Mac OS X 10.2 Update CD (as available via the Mac OS X Up-to-Date program) instead of the Install CD, it does not include the Archive and Install feature. Bummer.

2. Get permission

If you ever get an error message that says you cannot do something (typically move, delete, or open a file)—because you do not have sufficient permission—Jaguar's Finder now includes a way to work around almost all of these hassles. Previously, most solutions required either using Terminal or a shareware utility.

The Finder solution, assuming you are an administrator, is to select Get Info (Command-I) for the problem file and/or folder. From the Info window, go to the Ownership & Permissions section and make

yourself the owner, via the Owner pop-up menu. You should be able to do almost anything you want without getting the permissions error. If desired, you can revert back to the previous setting when you are done.

One caveat: Making changes to the contents of the /System folder or the Unix software is generally not recommended. Be cautious here.

3. Fix permissions

In some cases, permissions for software installed by Mac OS X (such as the files included in the /System folder) may get altered by mistake (a poorly written Installer package could do this, for example). In such cases, it would be nice if you could reset the permissions for all OS X software back to their defaults.

With Jaguar, you can. To do so, launch Disk Utility and select First Aid. Now click the Repair Disk Permissions button. This has no effect on third party software or on any files in the Users directory.

A tip: Disk Utility obtains its information about permissions settings from the Receipt files (in the /library/Receipts folder). Do not delete the files here. In fact, if your Receipts folder is empty, the options to Verify or Repair Disk Permissions are disabled!

4. Do a Safe Boot

Jaguar includes a Safe Boot procedure. It disables at startup all non-essential text files (stored in /System/Library/Extensions) and third-party Startup Items (located in /Library/StartupItems). This is useful if one of these items has become corrupt and is thus preventing a normal startup.

To perform a Safe Boot, hold down the Shift key at startup immediately after you hear the chimes. Keep holding it until the Mac logo appears on the screen. If you were successful, the words "Safe Boot" should now appear in the logo box. You can now release the Shift key.

The advantage of a Safe Boot is that it can circumvent a startup crash or kernel panic that one of these files might trigger if it tried to load. Once you have succeeded in starting up, you can locate the problem file and remove it from its folder (a utility such as MOX Optimize can help do this). If you have no idea which file is the culprit, suspect recently added and/or third-party files. Once you disable the culprit, you can restart normally. Contact the vendor of the file for further advice.

By the way, a carry-over from Mac OS X 10.1.3 or later, if you hold down the Shift key at the login window (after typing your password), you disable all items listed in the Login Items System Preference. This can help bypass a crash caused by one of these items..

5. Check Kernel panic logs

If you get a message that tells you (in several languages) that "You need to restart your computer. Hold down the Power button for several seconds or press the Restart button," you just got what is called a kernel panic. It is Mac OS X's equivalent of a system crash. As the message states, you need to restart. New in Jaguar, after a kernel panic occurs, details of what happened are recorded in the panic.log file in /Library/Logs. In general, the contents of this log file will only be intelligible to developers, helping them to debug the cause of the panic. However, if you are

technically-inclined, check out this Apple document which explains what the log text means:

http://developer.apple.com/technotes/tn2002/tn2063.html.

6. Check for red text in Force Quit window (or "Force Quit" text in Dock item)

New in Jaguar, if an application is frozen (not responding to any input and having an endlessly spinning cursor icon), the Force Quit window (accessed via Command-Option-Escape) displays the application's name in red, rather than black, text. This is a helpful way to confirm that the application truly is frozen, rather than just taking an unusually long time to complete a task.

Similarly, if you select the Dock menu for an application, the Quit item will automatically shift to Force Quit (no need to hold down the Option key), if the application is frozen. One advantage of selecting to Force Quit from the Dock menu is that it bypasses the Force Quit window. This may allow a Force Quit to succeed in situations where the Force Quit window is not responding.

7. Access CUPS from your browser

Apple overhauled the printing software in Jaguar to use something called CUPS (Common Unix Printing System). Print Center is now a front end for CUPS, but you can also access CUPS software directly by entering this URL in your browser: http://127.0.0.1:631/. From the CUPS Administration page that appears, you can do almost anything you can do from Print Center, plus some things you cannot do any other way. For example, you can select to print a test page from the CUPS Manage Printers page.

Of particular interest, click the Manage Jobs button from the main CUPS page. From here, click Show Completed Jobs. When you do this, you get a list of the names of all the documents you have printed. This information is stored in the page_log file in /var/log/cups. By editing the cupsd.conf file (in /etc/cups), you can adjust the maximum number of jobs that are preserved in page_log (MaxJobs; default is 500). You can similarly set whether or not to preserve the list of completed jobs at all (PreserveJobHistory; default is Yes).

8. Get third-party Menu Extras working

Apple changed Jaguar so that most third-party Menu Extras (those items that appear in the right hand side of the menu bar) no longer work. Happily, you can re-enable these banned Menu Extras via a utility called Menu Extra Enabler (www.unsanity.com/haxies/).

A few Menu Extras will still crash, even with Menu Extra Enabler installed. For these uncooperative items, an additional step is needed. Launch Terminal and type the following (the {space} text indicates potentially non-obvious places where a space exists):

sudo ln –s {space}
/System/Library/Frameworks/Application
Services.framework/Versions/A/Frameworks/
HIServices.framework {space}
/System/Library/PrivateFrameworks/HIService
s.framework

9. Fix Finder oddities by deleting plist and cache files

A variety of occasional problems in the Finder—such as applications that look like folders, applications that crash on launch, Finder menu commands that do not work, or an inability to get drag-and-drop to work—can be fixed by deleting one or more of an assortment of preferences (plist) and cache files that may have become corrupt.

If you don't want to be bothered hunting down and deleting these files yourself, there are several shareware utilities that automate the procedure for you. I especially recommend Dragster (http://www.ifthensoft.com/). It also provides a complete list of all the files/folders it will delete. Don't worry about trashing these files. New default copies are re-created automatically.

10. Search and view package contents

This last tip is not unique to Jaguar, but is still worth a mention.

The Finder's Find command does not search the contents of packages (files that end in pkg, such as installer package files). If you want to quickly search for a file that you believe is inside a package somewhere on your drive (but you are not sure where), a great solution is to use Locator (a front end for Unix's locate command). The simplest way to use it is to type "/" (root level) in the In text box; then enter the desired search text in the Locate text box.

A related tip: You can quickly navigate anywhere on your drive, including inside packages, by typing file://local in your Web browser. Each directory listed is a hypertext link to the contents of the directory (assuming you have permission to view it). As a bonus, the Web listing even shows normally invisible folders and files.

informIT

Photoshop® 7 with a Wacom® Tablet

Photoshop's behind-the-scenes photo editing power...

1. Dynamically change tool size

A Wacom pen tablet gives you the power to change the size of any of Photoshop's 20 pressure-sensitive tools with pen pressure. Press softly to get a thin stroke–press harder to get a thicker stroke. Here's the Clone Stamp set up to be pressure-sensitive for size–try out the other pressure-sensitive tools for fun! *(Visit our web site for a list of all 20 pressure-sensitive Photoshop tools.)*

2. Change tool opacity on the fly

Set the Paintbrush for Opacity, and you have Photoshop's most powerful tool for great layer masks! Paint lightly for a semi-transparent look, press harder for a clean knock-out. And when you're done with your Layer Mask, give the Art History brush a try–press lightly with your pen for transparent strokes, press harder for more opaque strokes.

3. Blend colors with your Paintbrush

Being able to change color during a brush stroke can give you some great effects. Set the Photoshop 7 Paintbrush to be color-sensitive in the Color Dynamics sub-palette and try it out. We've set the Paintbrush to be color-sensitive for an "organic" look as we colorize the black & white photo below with two different shades of peach.

4. Try a little tilt

Select the Shape Dynamics sub-palette and you can set the Angle to be affected by Pen Tilt. Modify a round brush to be an angular calligraphy brush, tilt the pen to the left or right and you'll get beautiful calligraphic brushstrokes. *(By the way, almost all of the pressure-sensitive tools are tilt-sensitive too!)*

5. A finger on the Wacom Airbrush

Wacom's Airbrush Pen now offers you a new method of control in Photoshop 7–the Fingerwheel. Grab the Wacom Airbrush, select the Photoshop Paintbrush, and you can set size, opacity, scatter, color and more to respond to the roll of the fingerwheel.

6. The comfort you need

The Intuos2 Grip Pen is built for comfort. It has a cushioned, contoured grip area and features Wacom's patented cordless, battery-free technology for a natural feel and superior performance.

7. Put it all together

Now imagine editing photographs with some of your favorite Photoshop techniques and the Wacom tablet. Control size and opacity with pressure to create accurate layer masks, burn and dodge quickly, and make subtle color corrections exactly where you want them.

For a FREE "Photoshop Power Tips" CD:

visit
www.macpowertips.com
or call
800-922-2584

Cintiq
Create Directly On Screen!
Cintiq starts at $1899

intuos2
Turn on Photoshop's power!
Intuos2 starts at $199

WACOM
www.wacom.com

NOTES

NOTES